SPECTRUM

Writing

Grade K

Published by Spectrum
an imprint of Carson-Dellosa Publishing LLC
Greensboro, NC

Spectrum is an imprint of Carson-Dellosa Publishing.

Send all inquiries to:
Carson-Dellosa Publishing
P.O. Box 35665
Greensboro, NC 27425

Printed in Madison, WI USA

ISBN 978-0-7696-8020-0

1 2 3 4 5 6 WCR 15 14 13 12 11

349108454

Table of Contents Grade K

Chapter 1 Writing Letters

Chapter 2 All About Me

Chapter 3 Story Words

Table of Contents, continued

NAME ______________________

Lesson 1 Letter Aa

acorn

Trace the letter **A**.

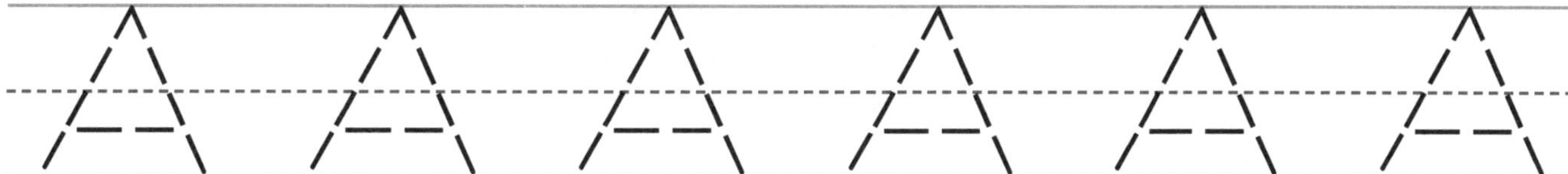

Write the letter **A**.

Trace the letter **a**.

Write the letter **a**.

NAME ______________________

Lesson 2 Letter Bb

Bb

basketball

Trace the letter **B**.

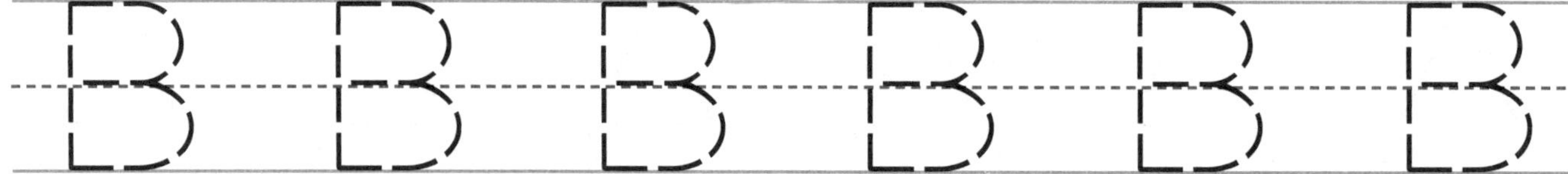

Write the letter **B**.

Trace the letter **b**.

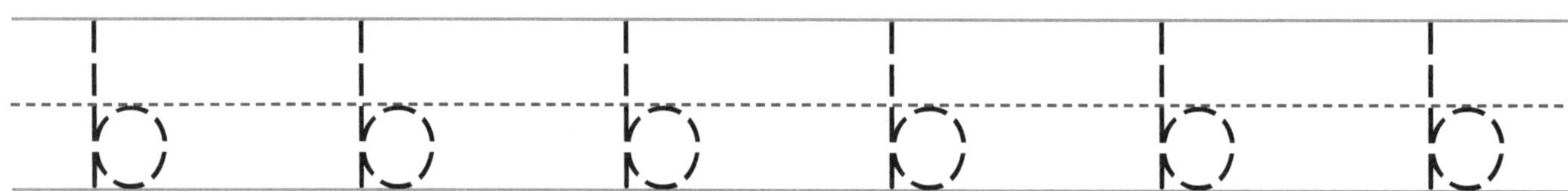

Write the letter **b**.

NAME ______________________

Lesson 3 Letter Cc

cat

Trace the letter **C**.

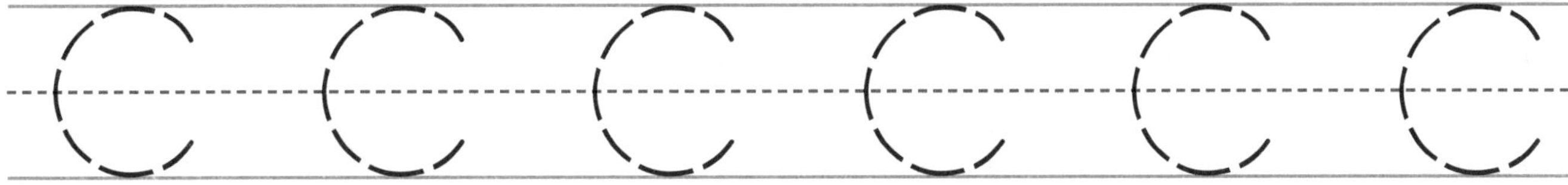

Write the letter **C**.

Trace the letter **c**.

Write the letter **c**.

NAME ______________________

Lesson 4 Letter Dd

Dd

Dr. Davis

dog

Trace the letter **D**.

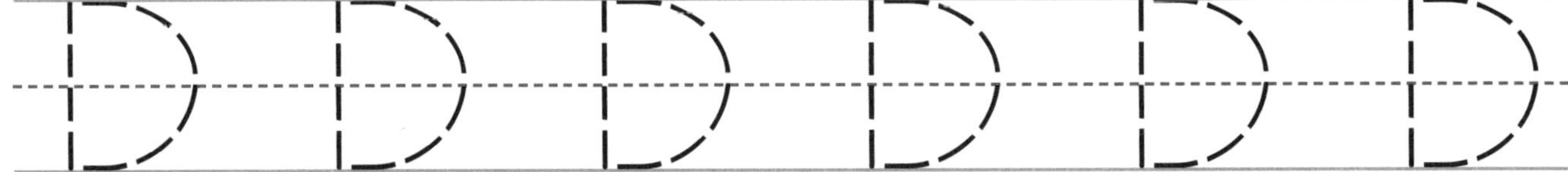

Write the letter **D**.

Trace the letter **d**.

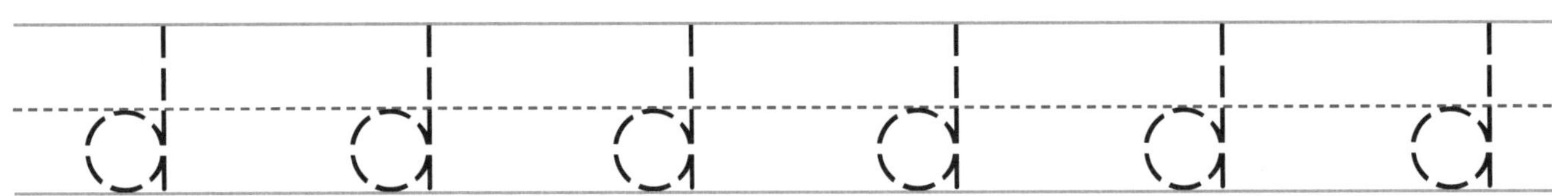

Write the letter **d**.

NAME ______________________________

Lesson 5 Letter Ee

Ee

egg

Trace the letter **E**.

Write the letter **E**.

Trace the letter **e**.

Write the letter **e**.

NAME ______________________

Lesson 6 Letter Ff

Ff

Trace the letter **F**.

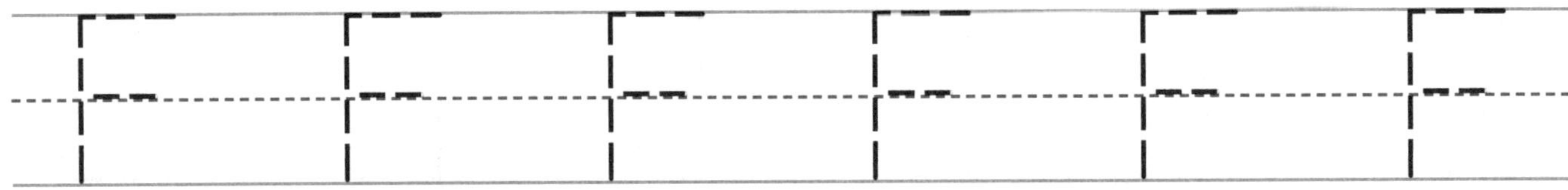

Write the letter **F**.

Trace the letter **f**.

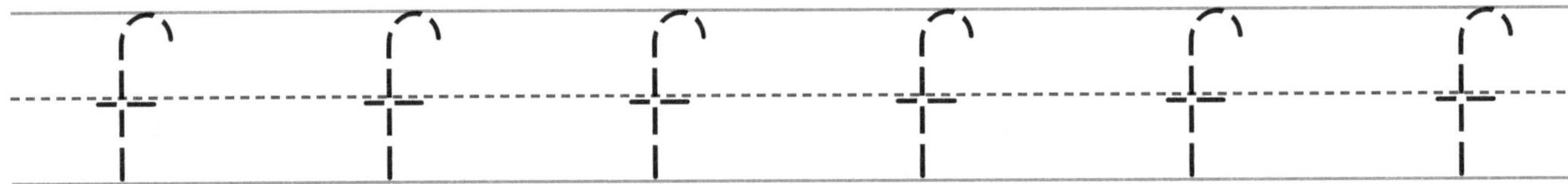

Write the letter **f**.

NAME ____________________

Review Letters Aa–Ff

Trace and write each letter.

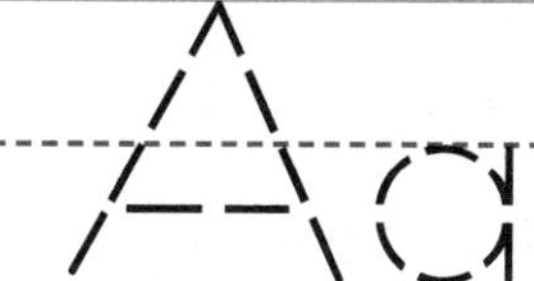

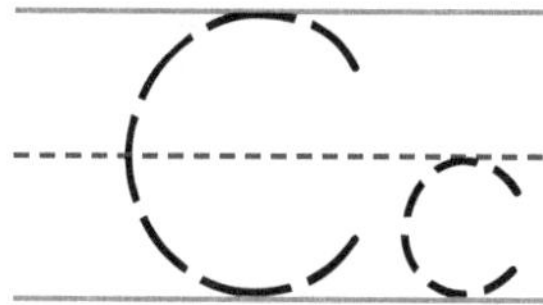

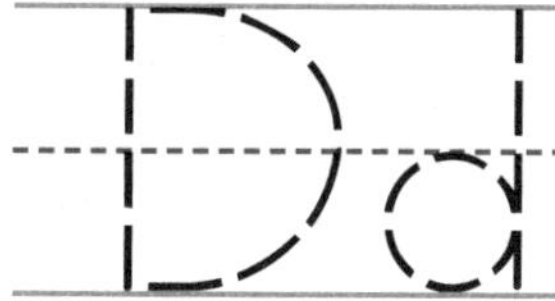

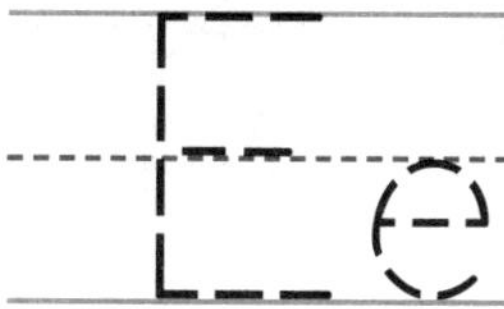

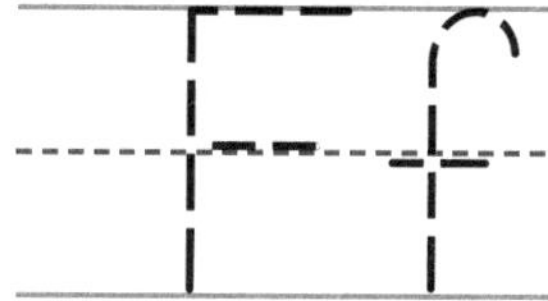

NAME ____________________

Lesson 7 Letter Gg

goose

Trace the letter **G**.

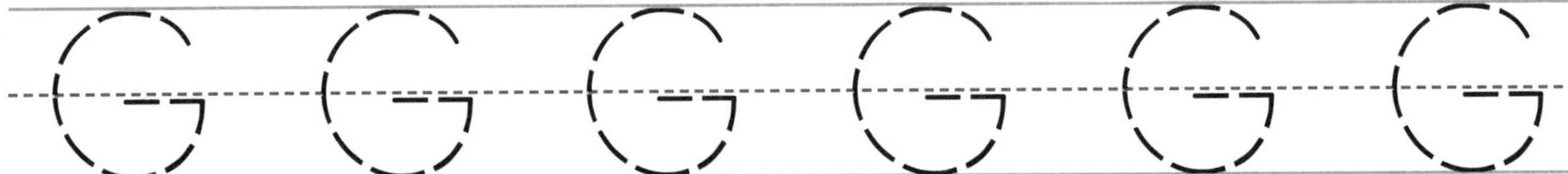

Write the letter **G**.

Trace the letter **g**.

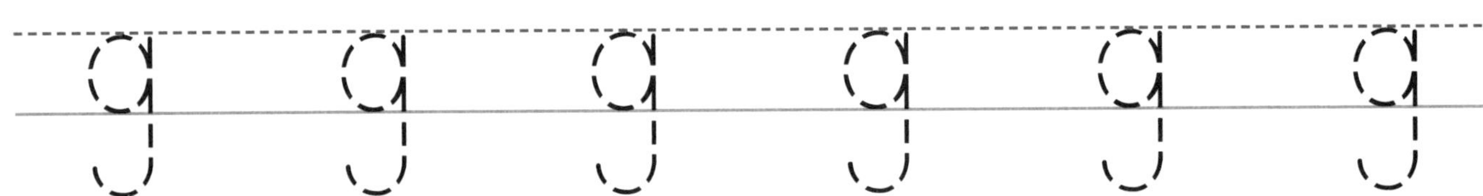

Write the letter **g**.

NAME ___________________________

Lesson 8 Letter Hh

hat

Trace the letter **H**.

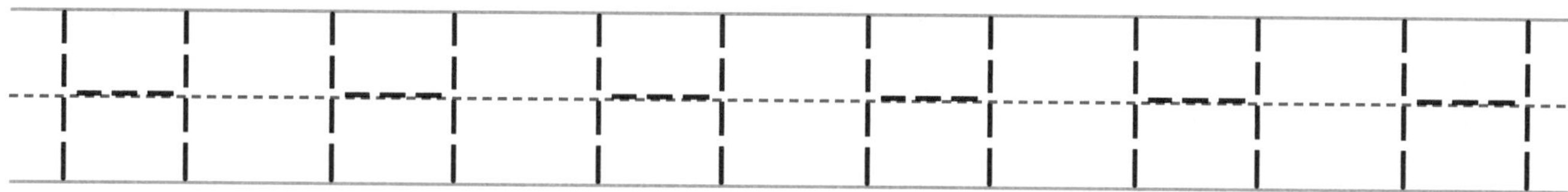

Write the letter **H**.

Trace the letter **h**.

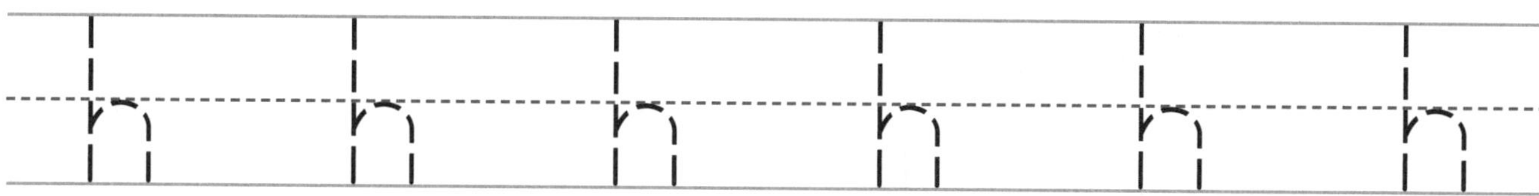

Write the letter **h**.

NAME ______________________

Lesson 9 Letter Ii

Ivy

igloo

Trace the letter **I**.

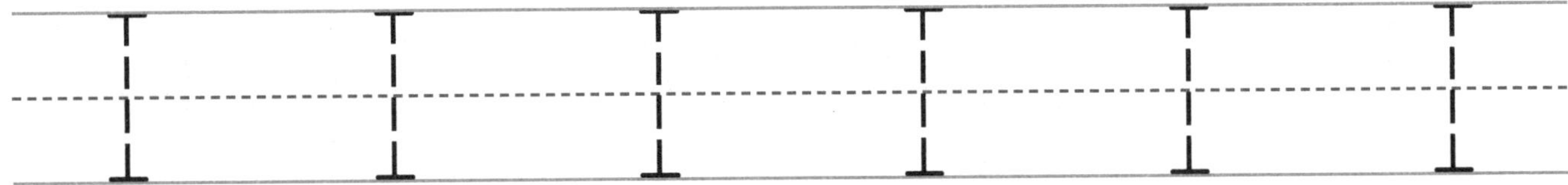

Write the letter **I**.

Trace the letter **i**.

Write the letter **i**.

NAME ______________________

Lesson 10 Letter Jj

Jj

jam

Trace the letter **J**.

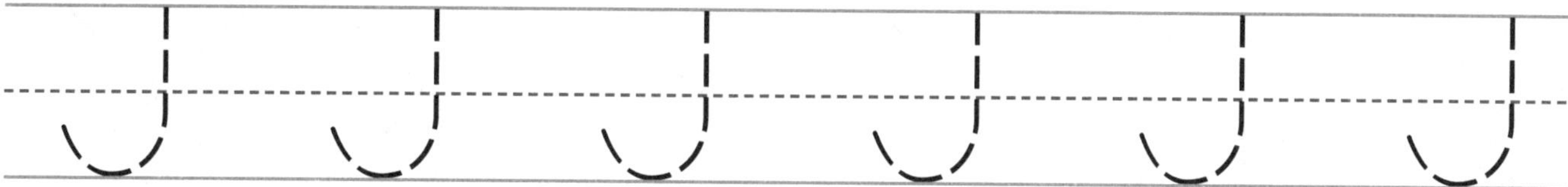

Write the letter **J**.

Trace the letter **j**.

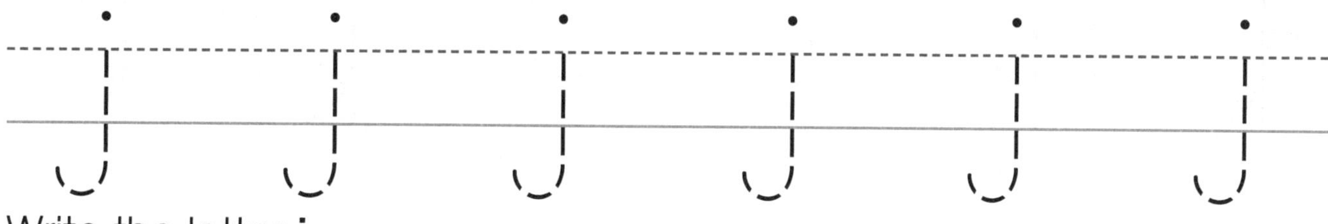

Write the letter **j**.

NAME ______________________

Lesson 11 Letter Kk

Kk

kangaroo

Trace the letter **K**.

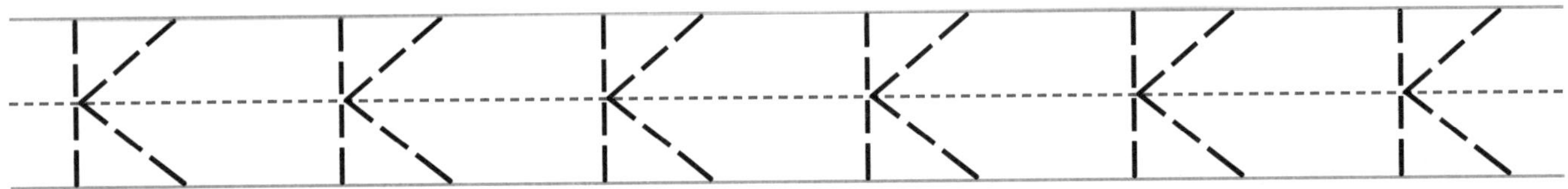

Write the letter **K**.

Trace the letter **k**.

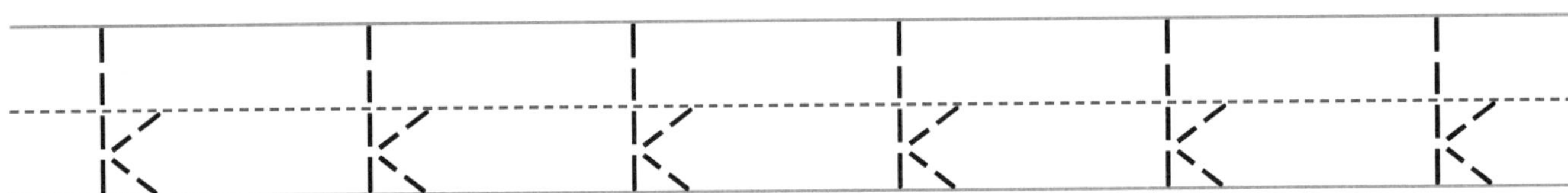

Write the letter **k**.

NAME ______________________

Lesson 12 Letter Ll

leaf

Trace the letter **L**.

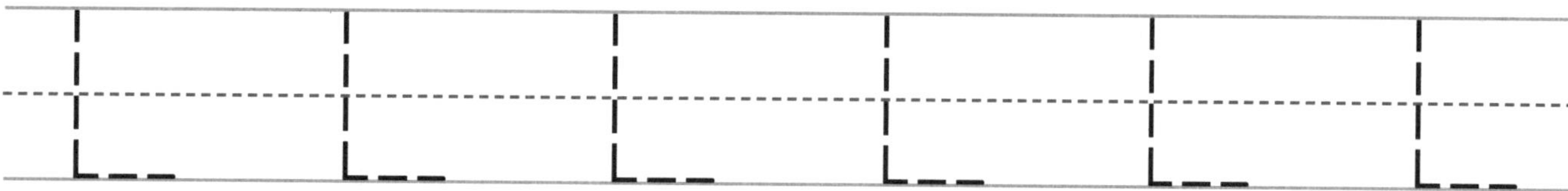

Write the letter **L**.

Trace the letter **l**.

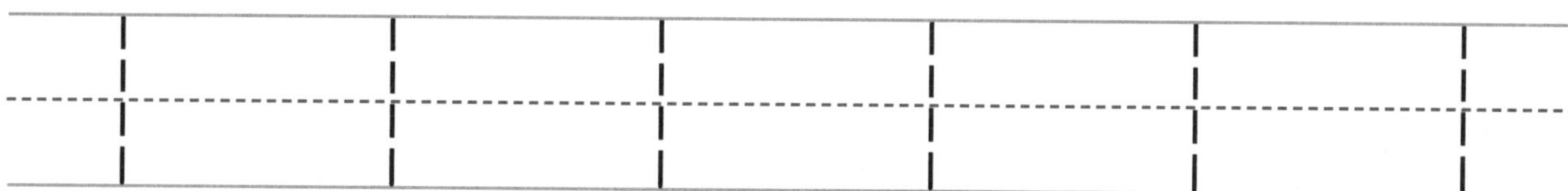

Write the letter **l**.

NAME ____________________

Review Letters Gg–Ll

Trace and write each letter.

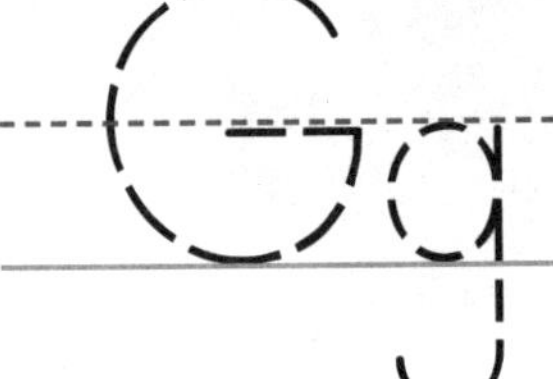

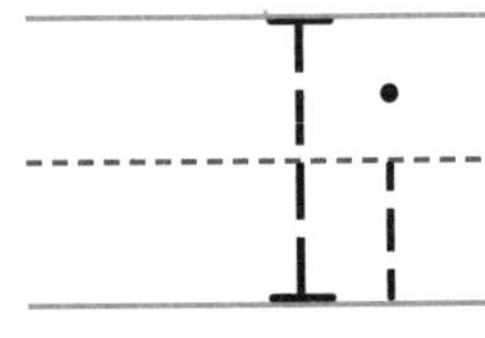

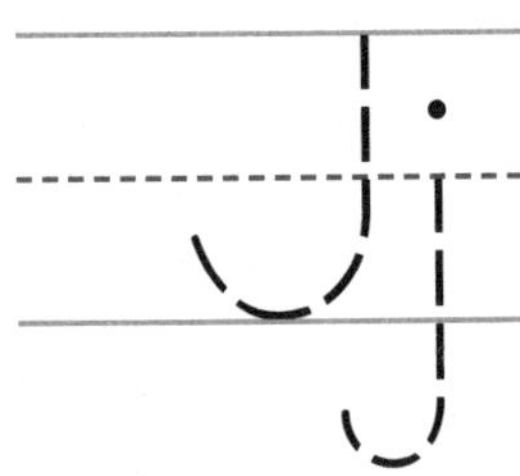

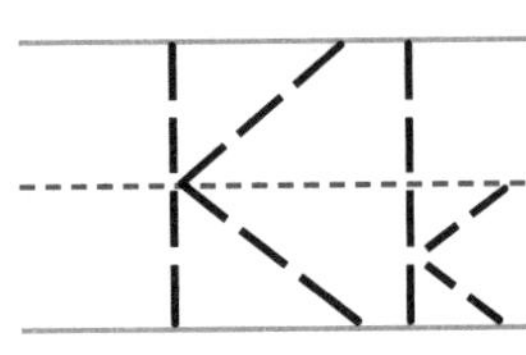

NAME ______________________

Lesson 13 Letter Mm

Mm

Mr. Mack **mouse**

Trace the letter **M**.

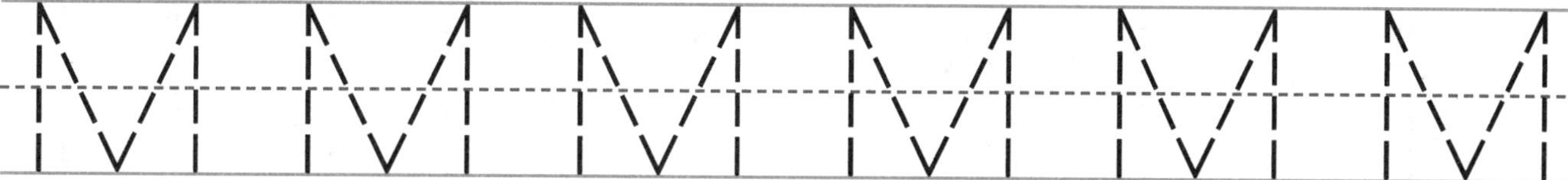

Write the letter **M**.

Trace the letter **m**.

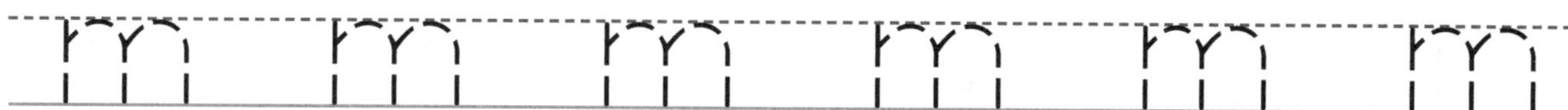

Write the letter **m**.

NAME ______________________

Lesson 14 Letter Nn

Nn

nut

Trace the letter **N**.

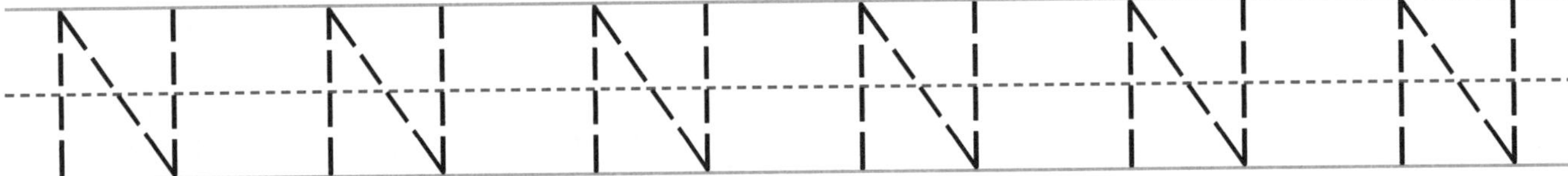

Write the letter **N**.

Trace the letter **n**.

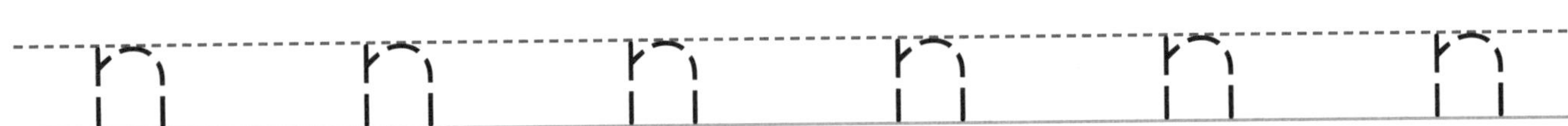

Write the letter **n**.

NAME ___________________________

Lesson 15 Letter Oo

octopus

Trace the letter **O**.

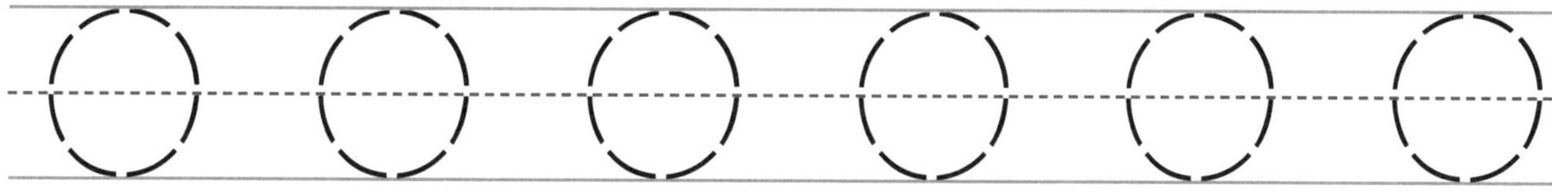

Write the letter **O**.

Trace the letter **o**.

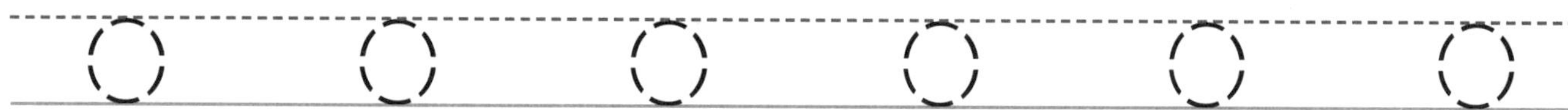

Write the letter **o**.

NAME ____________________

Lesson 16 Letter Pp

Pig

Trace the letter **P**.

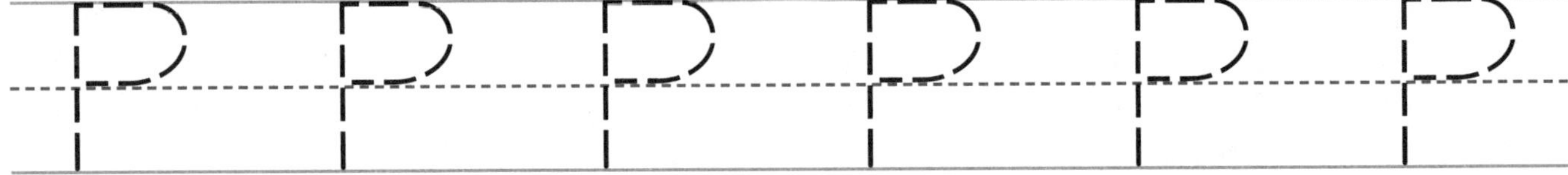

Write the letter **P**.

Trace the letter **p**.

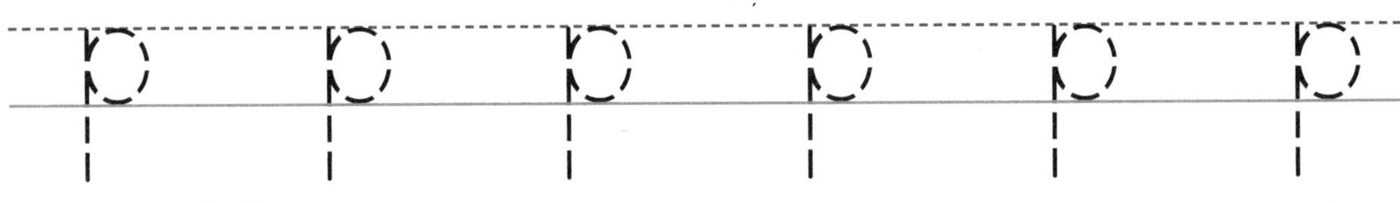

Write the letter **p**.

NAME ____________________

Lesson 17 Letter Qq

Qq

quarter

Trace the letter **Q**.

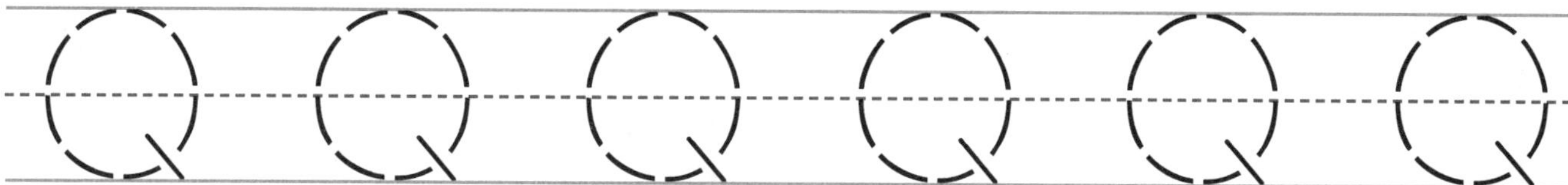

Write the letter **Q**.

Trace the letter **q**.

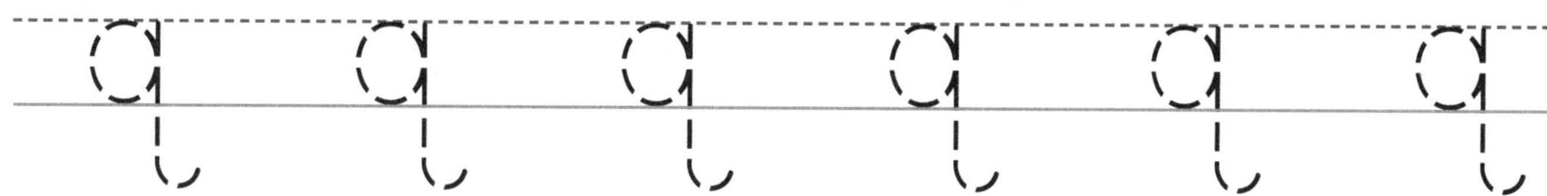

Write the letter **q**.

NAME ______________________

Lesson 18 Letter Rr

ring

Trace the letter **R**.

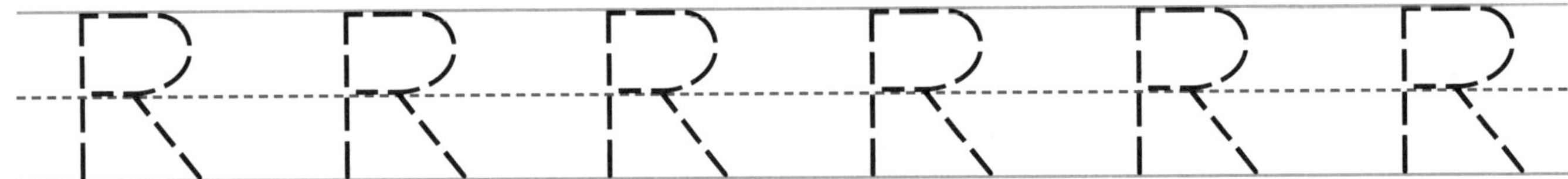

Write the letter **R**.

Trace the letter **r**.

Write the letter **r**.

NAME ____________________

Lesson 19 Letter Ss

Ss

sun

Trace the letter **S**.

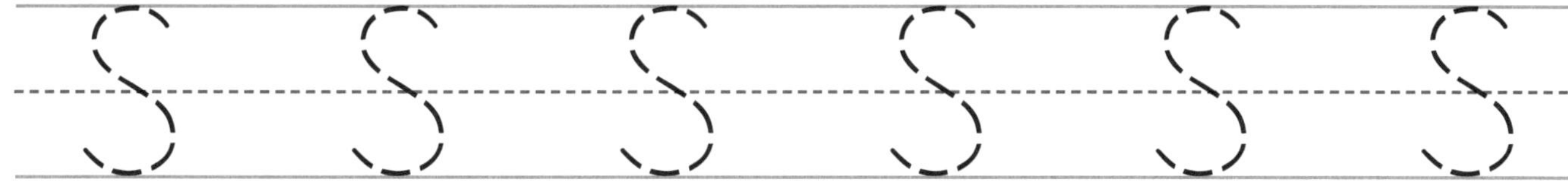

Write the letter **S**.

Trace the letter **s**.

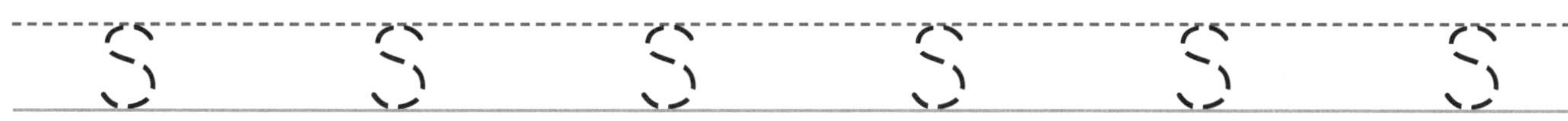

Write the letter **s**.

NAME ____________________

Review Letters Mm–Ss

Trace and write each letter.

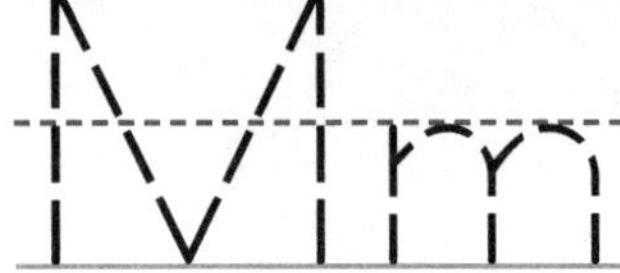

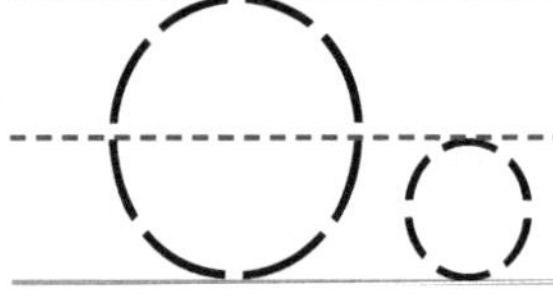

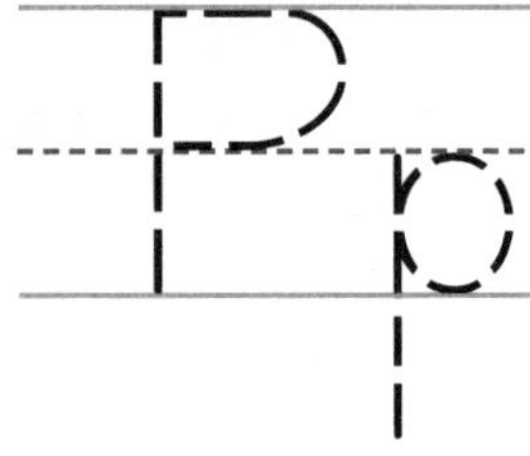

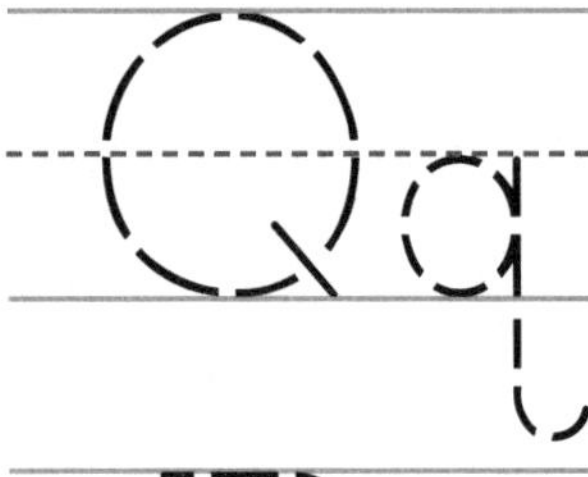

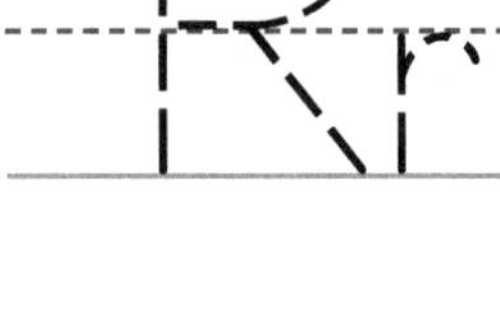

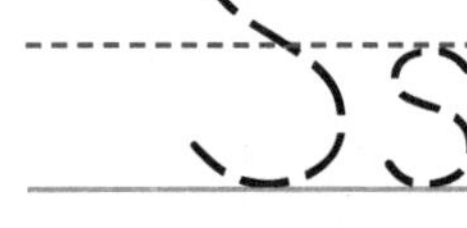

NAME ______________________

Lesson 20 Letter Tt

turtle

Trace the letter **T**.

Write the letter **T**.

Trace the letter **t**.

Write the letter **t**.

NAME ____________________

Lesson 21 Letter Uu

Uu

umbrella

Trace the letter **U**.

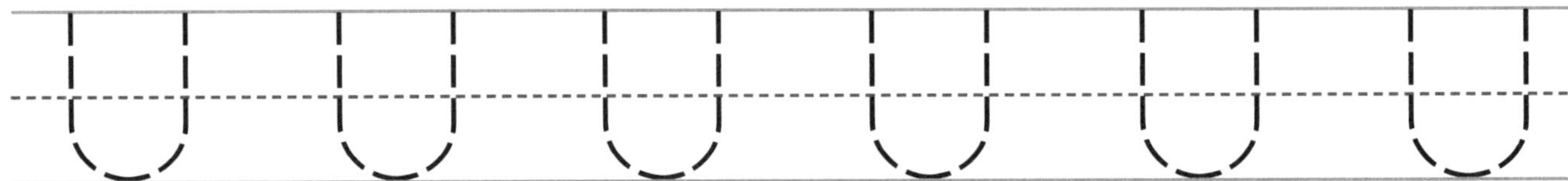

Write the letter **U**.

Trace the letter **u**.

Write the letter **u**.

NAME ___________________________

Lesson 22 Letter Vv

violin

Trace the letter **V**.

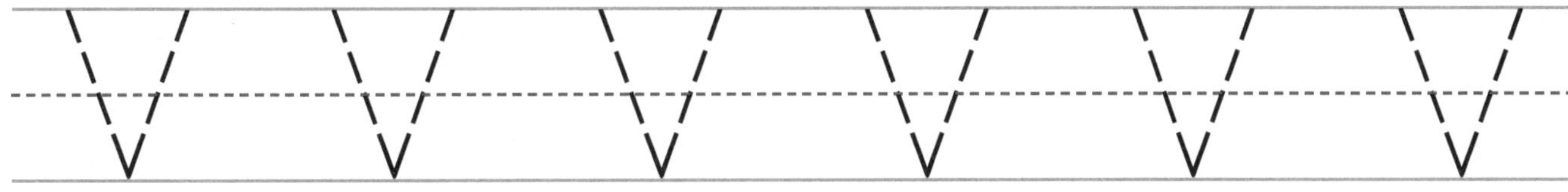

Write the letter **V**.

Trace the letter **v**.

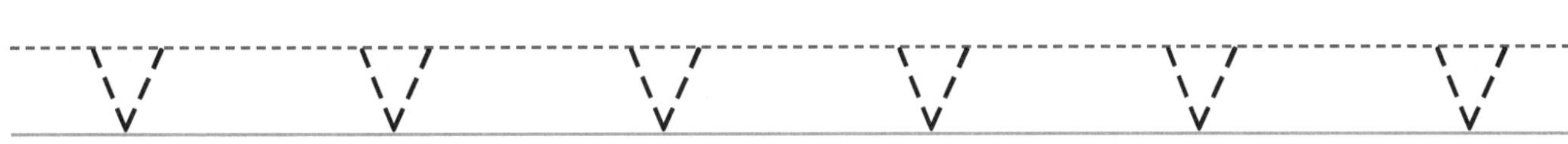

Write the letter **v**.

NAME ______________________

Lesson 23 Letter Ww

web

Trace the letter **W**.

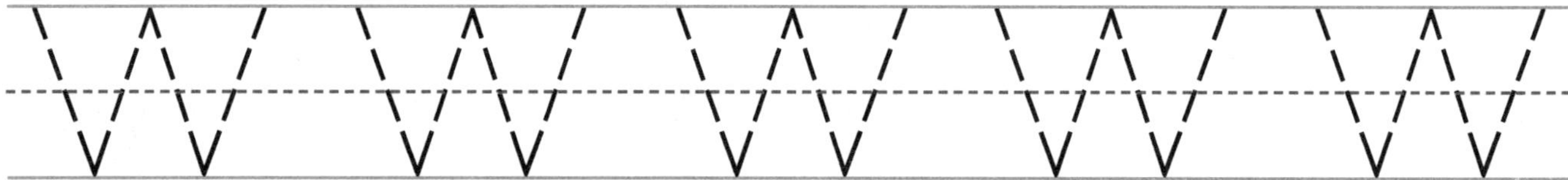

Write the letter **W**.

Trace the letter **w**.

Write the letter **w**.

NAME ____________________

Lesson 24 Letter Xx

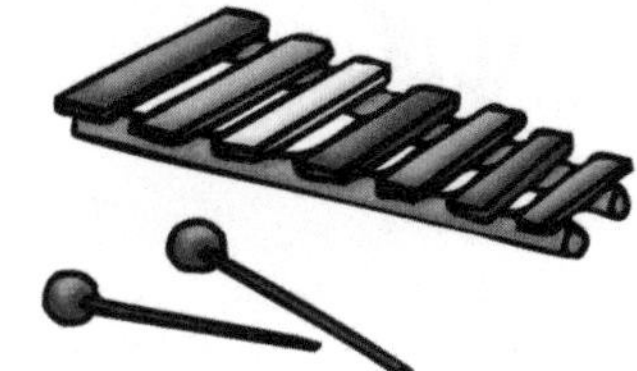

xylophone

Trace the letter **X**.

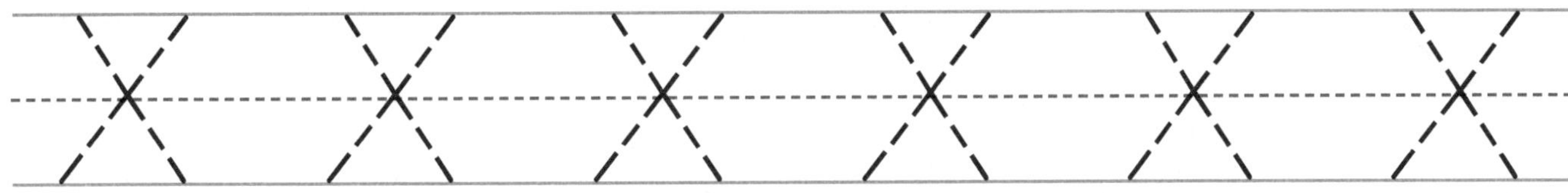

Write the letter **X**.

Trace the letter **x**.

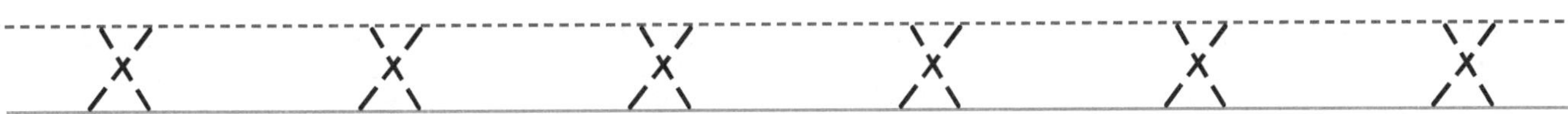

Write the letter **x**.

NAME ______________________

Lesson 25 Letter Yy

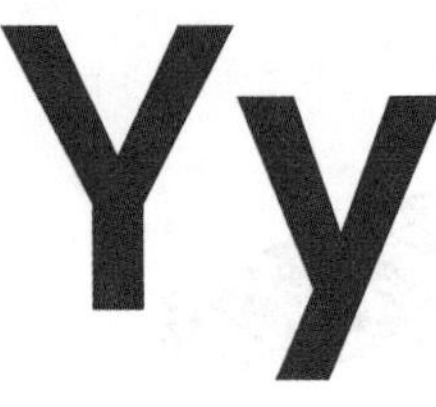

yo-yo

Trace the letter **Y**.

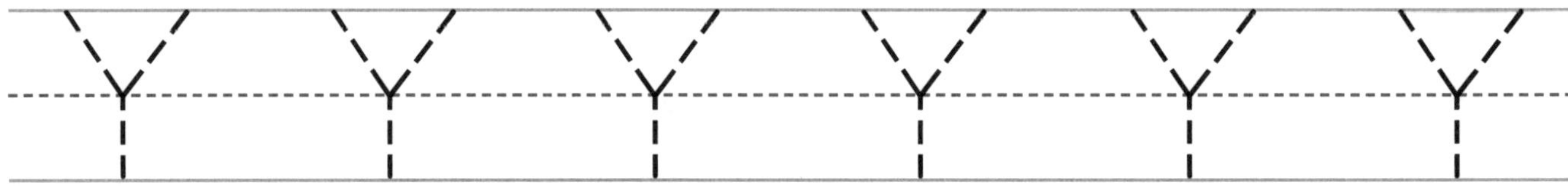

Write the letter **Y**.

Trace the letter **y**.

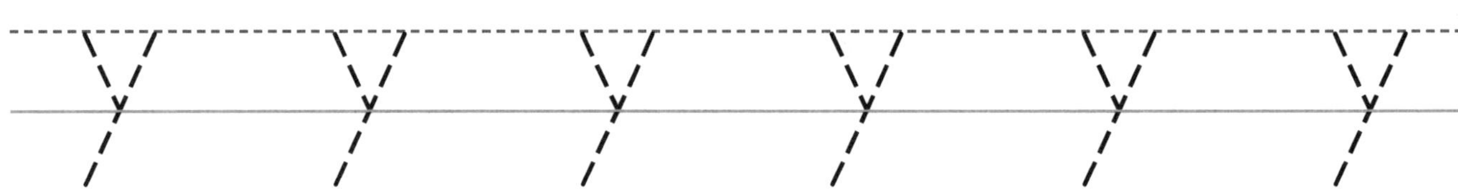

Write the letter **y**.

NAME ________________

Lesson 26 Letter Zz

Zz

zebra

Trace the letter **Z**.

Write the letter **Z**.

Trace the letter **z**.

Write the letter **z**.

NAME ____________________

Review Letters Tt–Zz

Trace and write each letter.

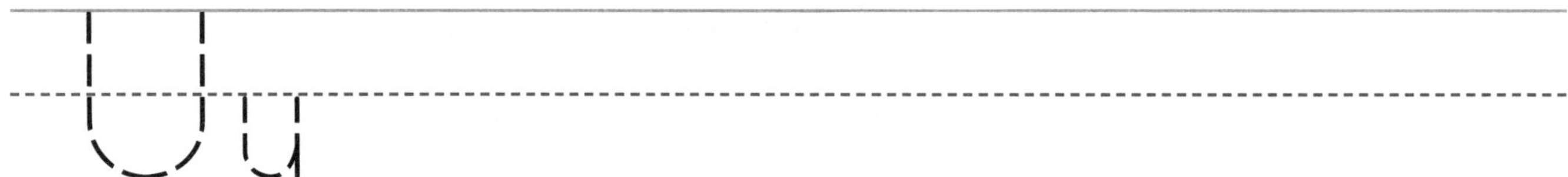

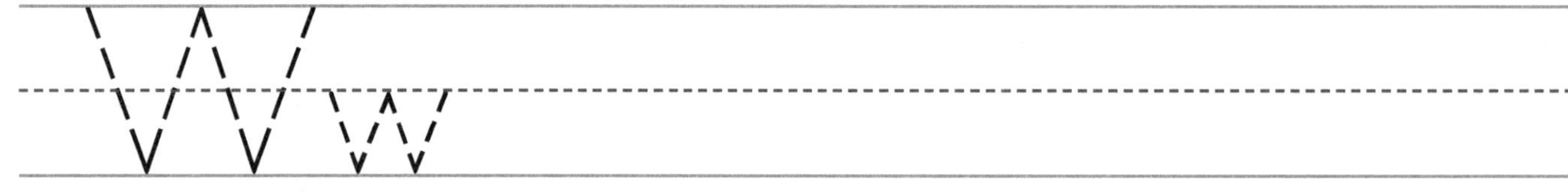

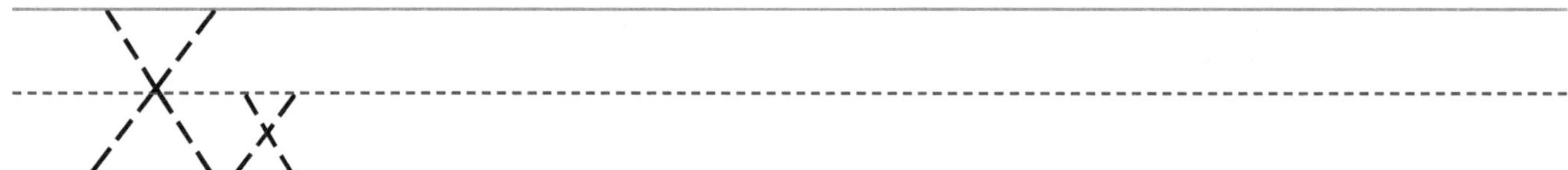

NAME ______________________________

Chapter 1 Post-Test

Connect the dots in ABC order to find what goes up.

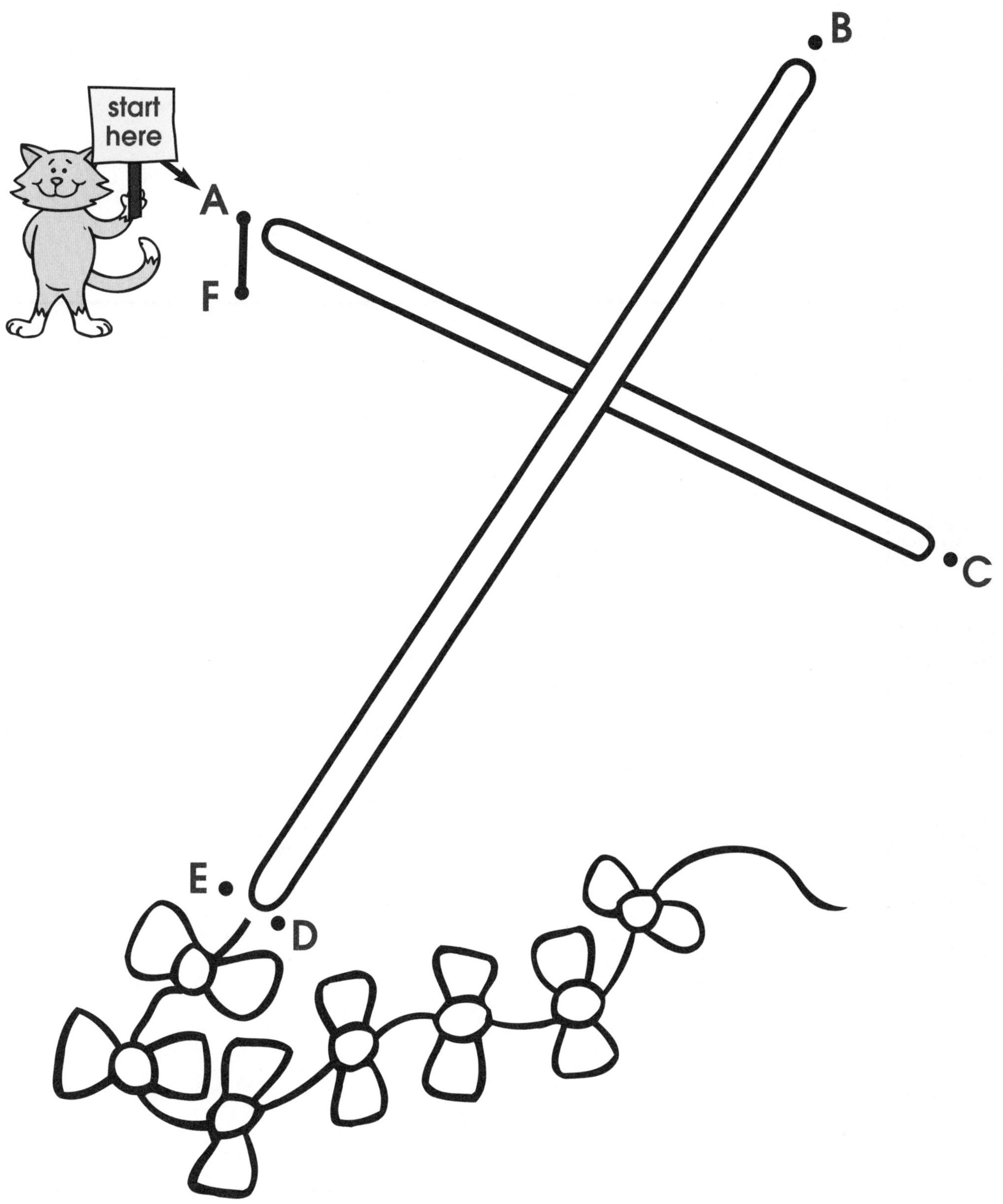

Chapter 2

NAME ______________________

Lesson 1 My Name

Write your name. Then, draw a picture of yourself.

My name is

____

NAME ______________________

Lesson 2 My Pet

Write the name of your pet. Then, draw a picture of it.

My pet's name is

____ .

NAME ______________________

Lesson 3 My Favorite Food

Write the name of your favorite food. Then, draw it in the box.

My favorite food is

____.

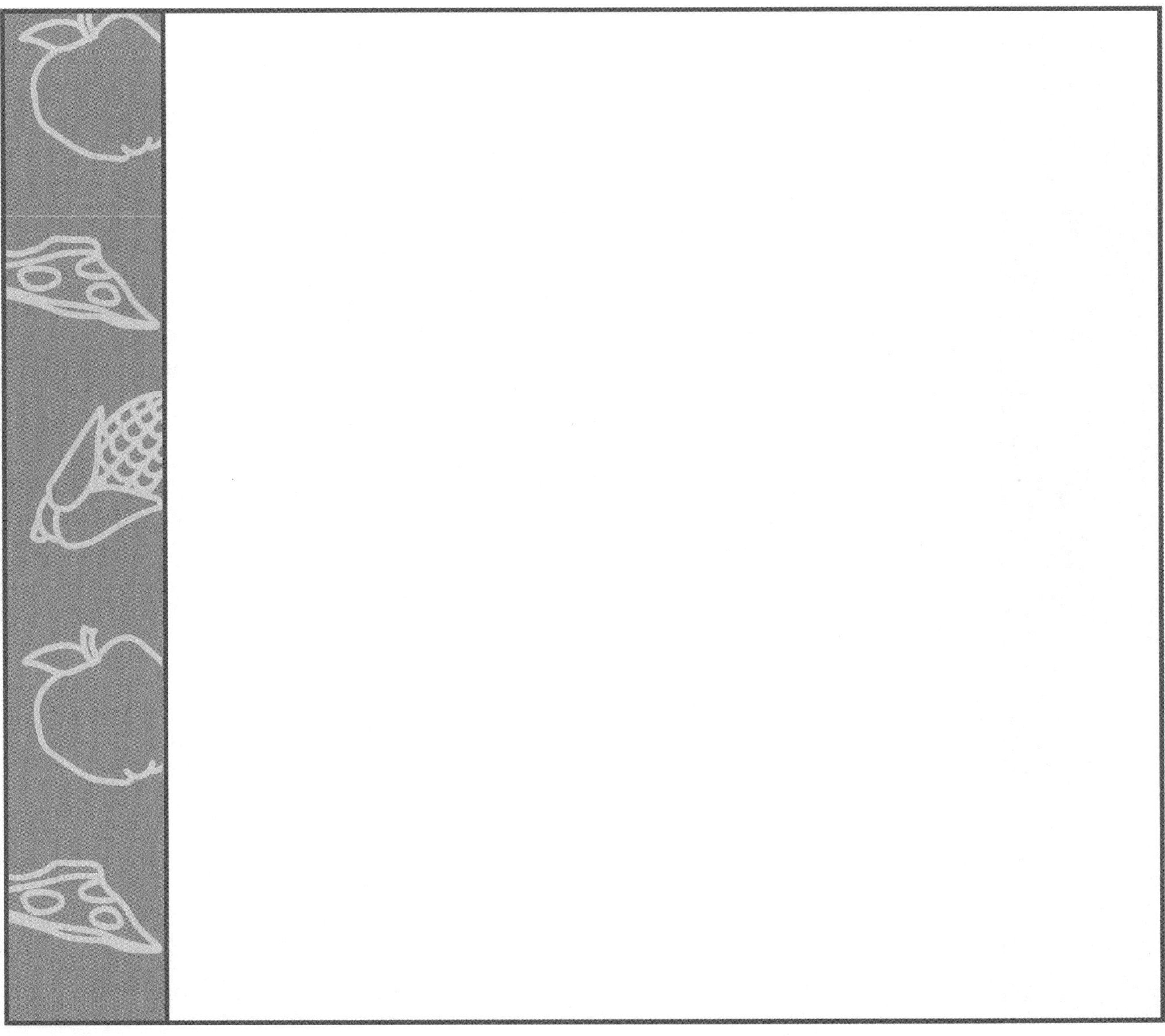

NAME ____________________

Lesson 4 My Favorite Toy

Write it the name of your favorite toy. Then, draw it in the box.

My favorite toy is

NAME ____________________

Lesson 5 My Teacher

Write the name of your teacher. Then, draw a picture of your teacher.

My teacher's name is

______________________________________.

NAME ____________________

Lesson 6 My Friend

Write your friend's name. Then, draw a picture of your friend.

My friend's name is

____.

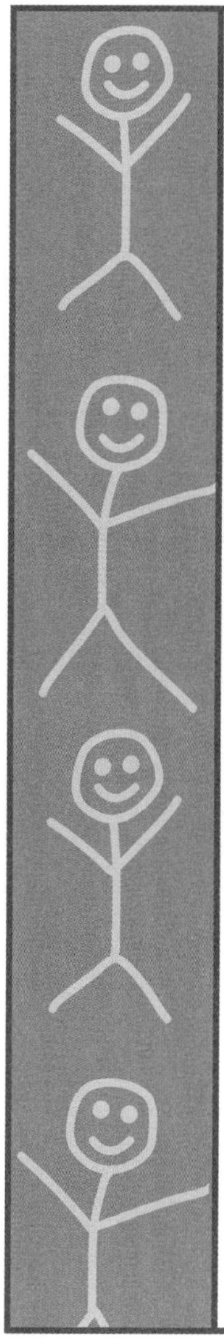

NAME ____________________

Lesson 7 My Family

Write the names of the people in your family. Then, draw your family.

The names of the people in my family are

NAME ______________________________

Lesson 8 My Home

Write your address. Then, draw your home.

My address is

____

____

______________________________ .

NAME ______________________________

Chapter 2 Post-Test

Write about something you like to do. Then, draw yourself doing it.

I like to

____

____.

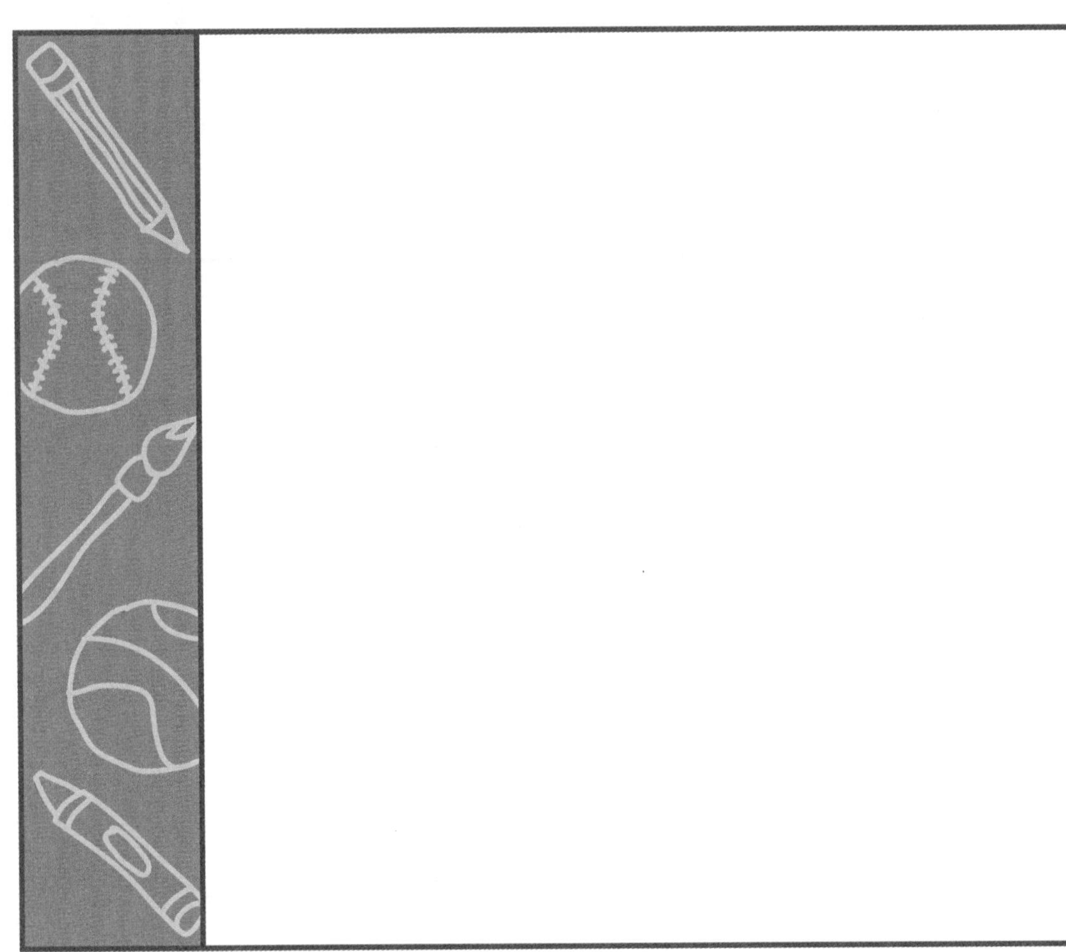

Chapter 3

NAME ___________________________

Lesson 1 Color Words

Trace and write each color word.

blue

yellow

green

red

orange

purple

NAME ________________________

Lesson 1 Color Words

Write the word from the box that names the color of each picture.

red	green	blue	yellow	purple	orange

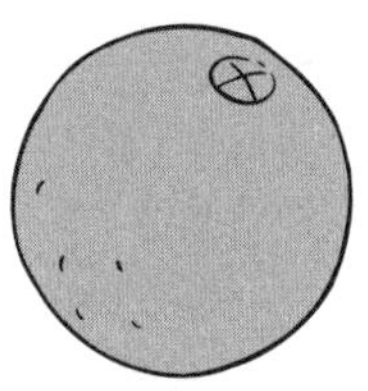

NAME ______________________

Lesson 2 Shape Words

Trace and write each shape word.

circle

triangle

rectangle

square

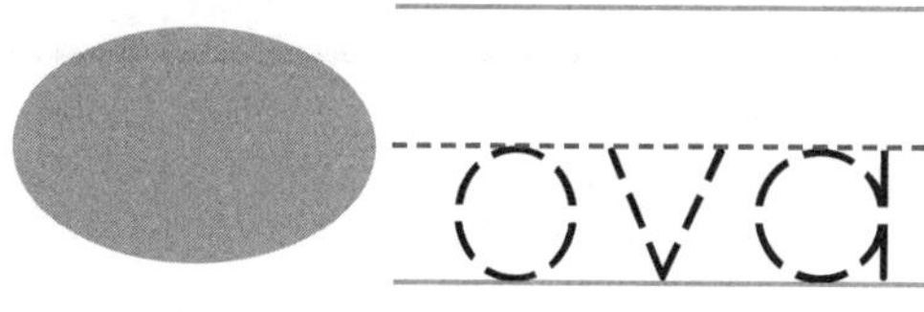

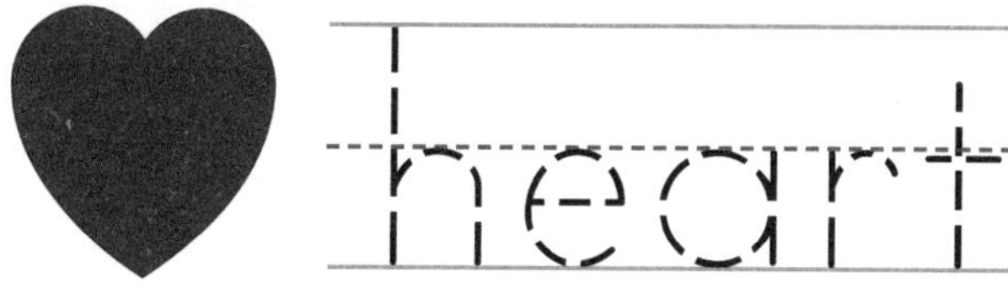

NAME ______________________

Lesson 2 Shape Words

Write the word that names each shape.

circle	oval	square	rectangle	triangle	heart

NAME ______________________

Lesson 3 Number Words

Number words tell how many.

Count the stars. Trace the number word. Write the word.

one

two

three

four

NAME ___________________

Lesson 3 Number Words

Number words tell how many.

Count the stars. Trace the number word. Write the word.

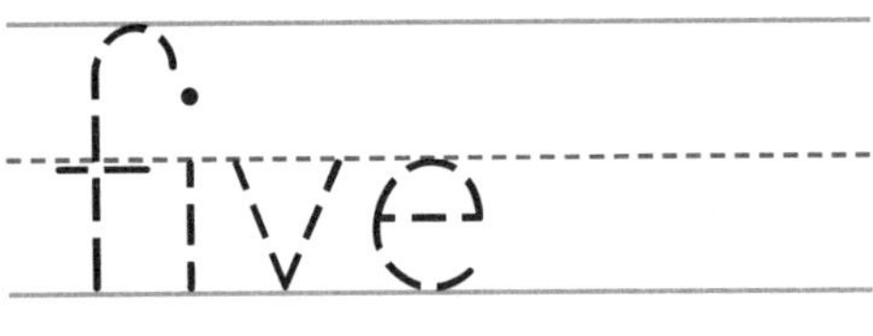

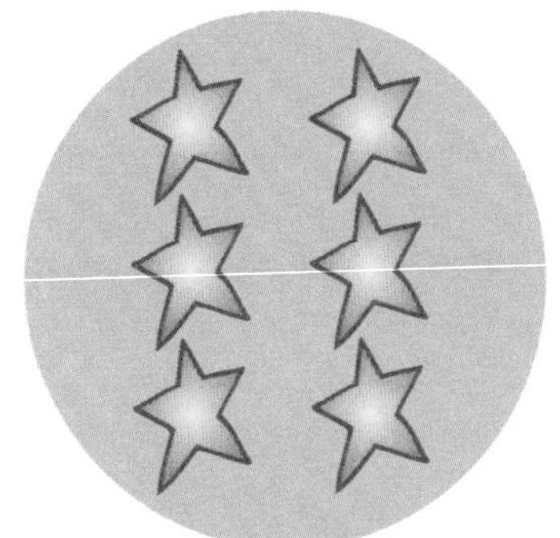

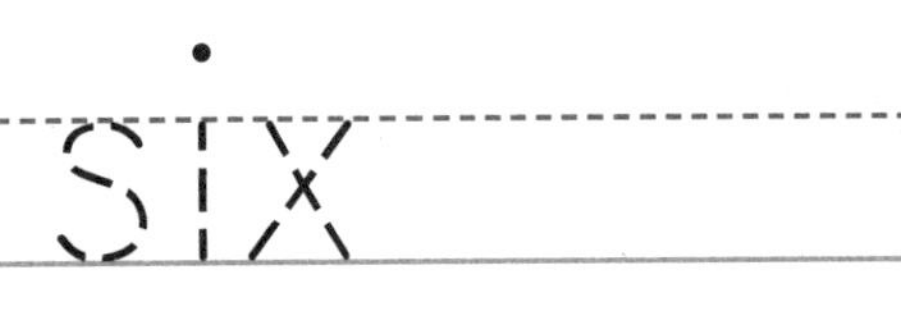

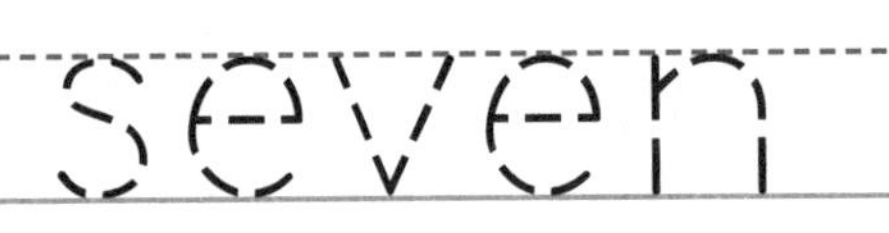

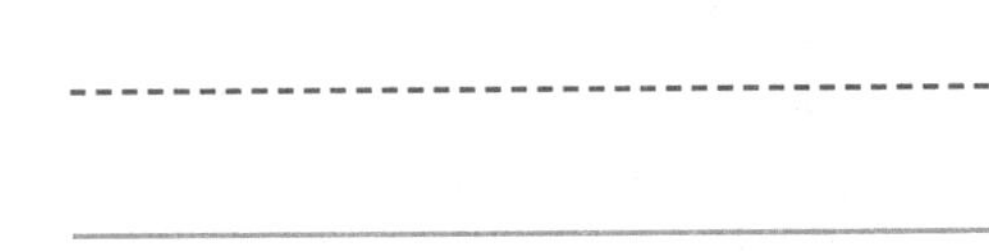

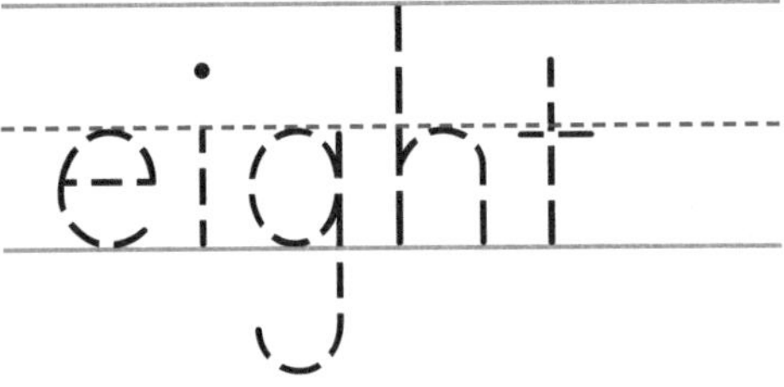

NAME ______________________

Lesson 4 Size Words

Trace and write each size word.

The dinosaur is big. ______

The mouse is . ______

The tree is . ______

The bush is short. ______

NAME ____________________

Lesson 4 Size Words

Write the correct size word on each line.

tall **short**

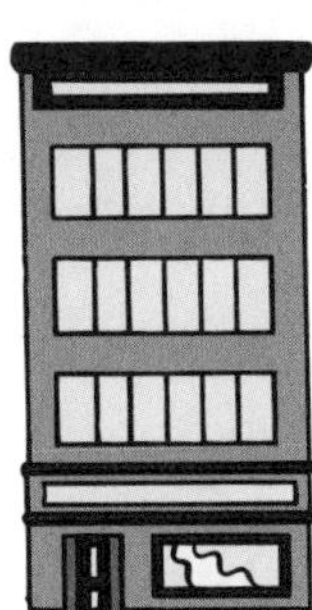

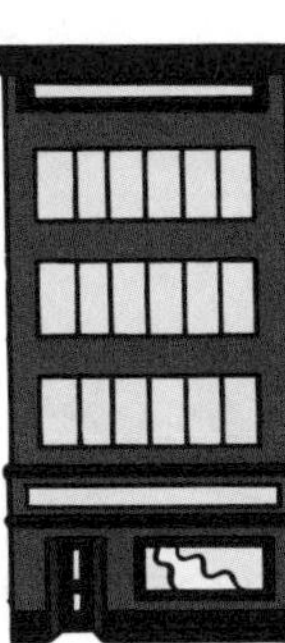

big **small**

Draw something tall.

Draw something small.

NAME ______________________

Review

Trace each color name. Then, color each shape correctly.

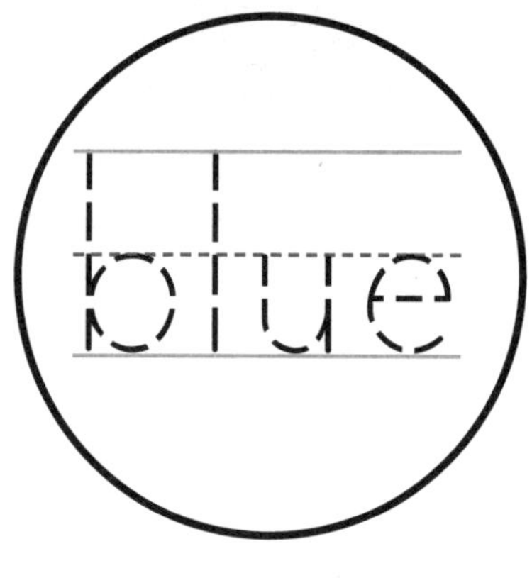

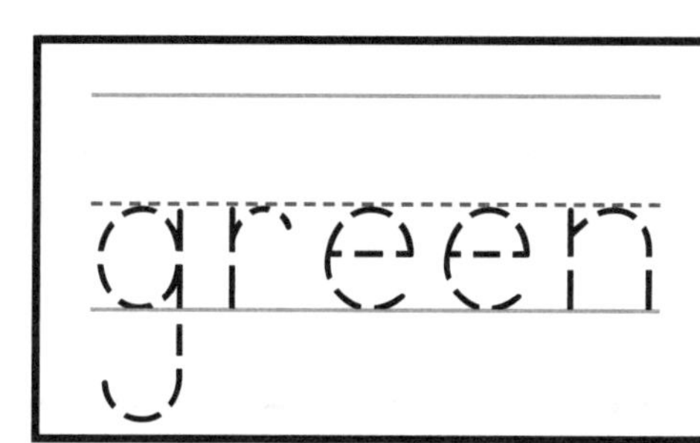

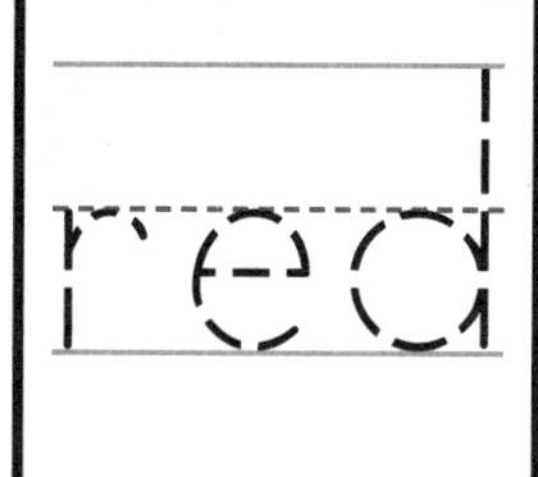

Draw a line from each shape to its name. Then, trace each name.

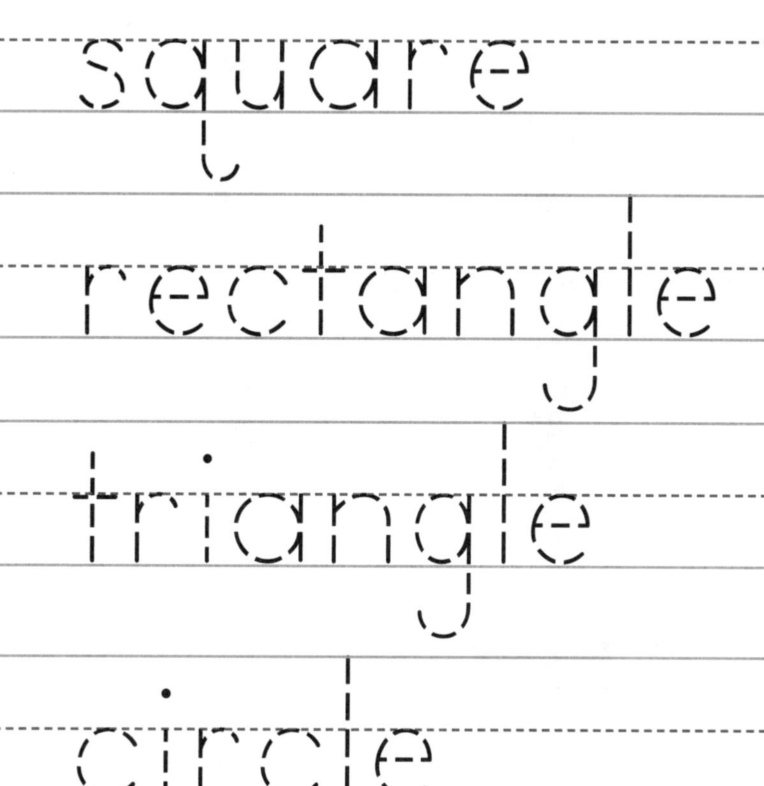

NAME ____________________

Review

Count the balloons. Then, write the number on the line.

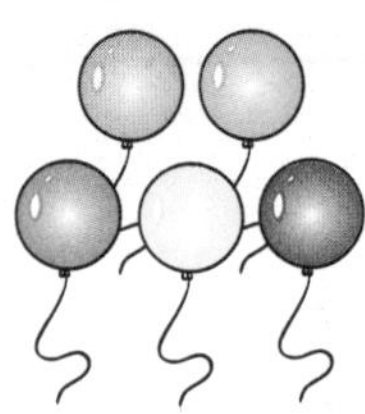

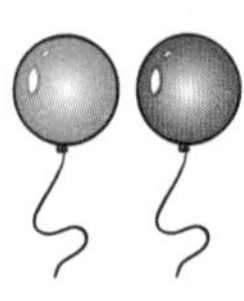

Circle the **big** tiger. Then, write **big**.

Circle the **short** tree. Then, write **short**.

Circle the **tall** man. Then, write **tall**.

Circle the **small** sandwich. Then, write **small**.

NAME ______________________

Lesson 5 Naming Words

A naming word names a person, place, or thing.

Trace and write each naming word.

person

place

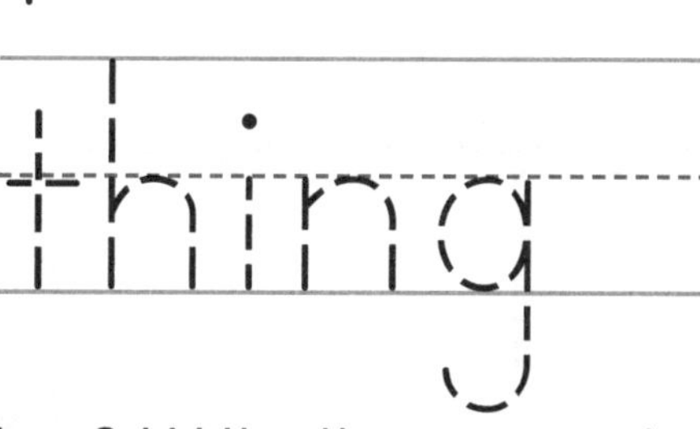

thing

Person? Place? Thing? Write the correct answer.

Lesson 5 Naming Words

Write the correct naming word under each picture.

person	place	thing

____

____

____

____

____

NAME ______________________

Lesson 6 Action Words

Action words show movement.

Trace each action word.

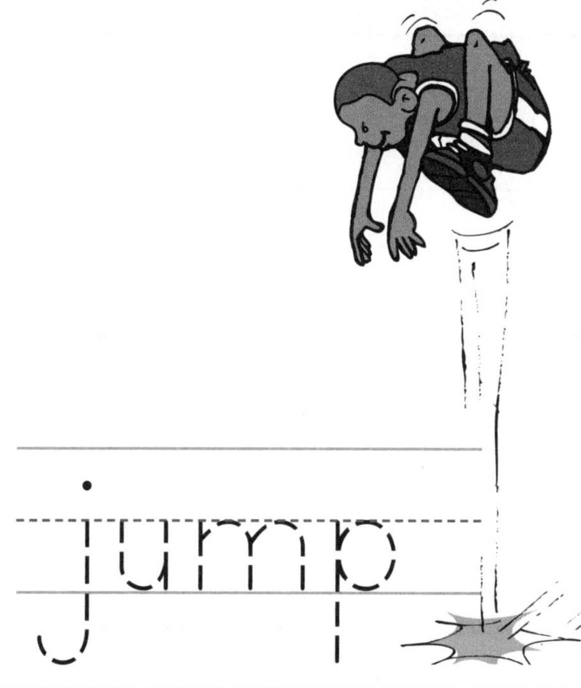

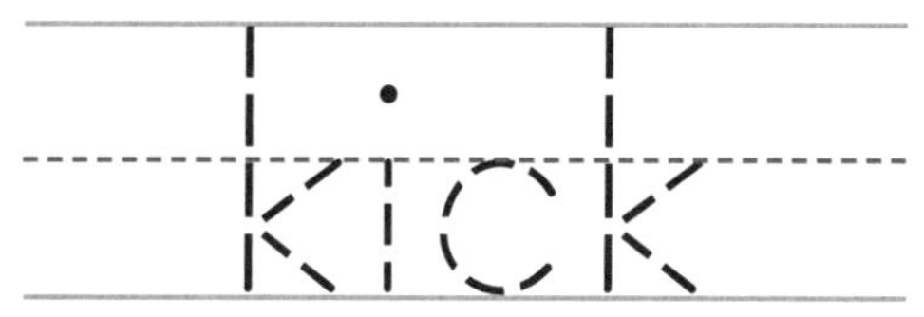

NAME ______________________

Lesson 6 Action Words

Write the action word that goes with each picture.

run	throw	kick	jump

Which action do you like to do?

NAME ______________________

Lesson 7 Position Words

Position words tell where things are located.

Trace and write each position word.

The boy is in the bed. ______

Fluffy is jumping over the mouse. ______

The mouse is on the drum. ______

The calf is beside the cow. ______

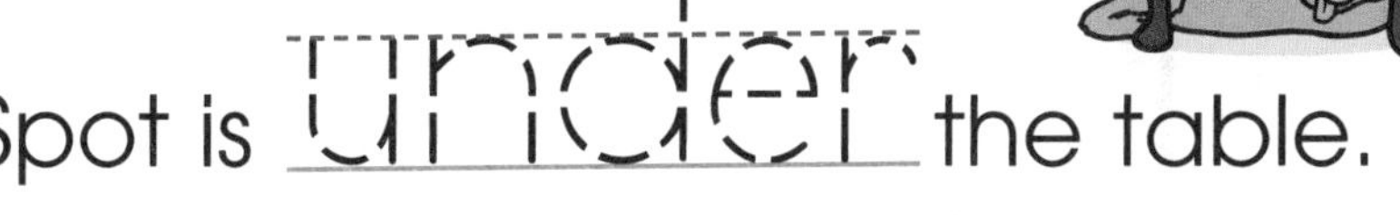

Spot is under the table. ______

NAME ____________________

Lesson 7 Position Words

Write the correct position word to show where the mouse is.

under	over	in	beside	on

Draw a worm in an apple.

NAME ______________________

Lesson 8 Describing Words

Describing words tell how things look or feel.

Trace and write each describing word.

The movie made Lauren 

. ______________

José is a 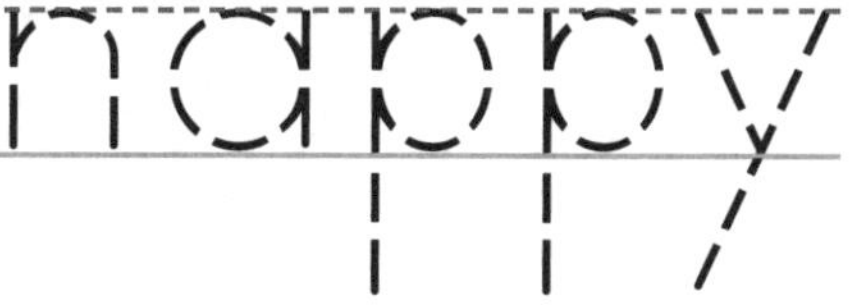

boy. ______________

The rabbit is very soft. ______________

My bat is hard. ______________

NAME ______________________

Lesson 8 Describing Words

Write the describing word that tells about each picture.

happy	hard	sad	soft

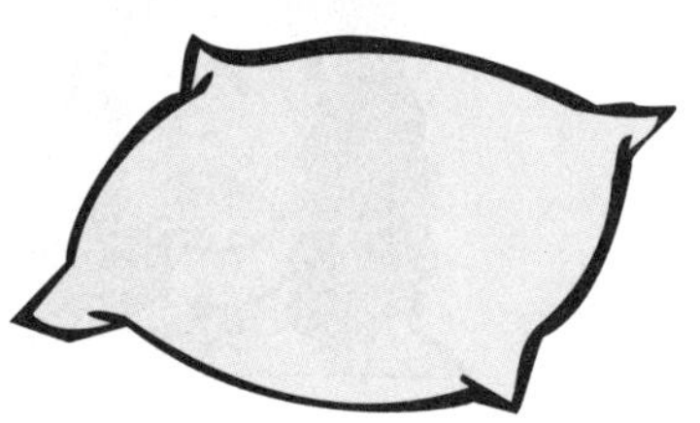

The pillow is ______________ .

This is a ______________ face.

My desk is ______________ .

The story made me ______________ .

NAME ______________________

Lesson 9 Order Words

Order words tell the order in which things happen.

Trace and write each order word.

, get your paper and crayons. ______________________

Next, draw your picture. ______________________

Last, hang up your picture. ______________________

NAME ______________________

Lesson 9 Order Words

Write the describing word that goes with each picture.

first	next	last

______________ Lauren gets a hammer, nails, and wood.

______________ Lauren hangs the birdhouse in a tree.

______________ Lauren makes a birdhouse.

NAME ____________________

Review

Write the correct naming word to complete each sentence.

Naming Words

- person
- place
- thing

The diving board is a ____________________.

The girl is a ____________________.

The pool is a ____________________.

Write the correct action word to complete each sentence.

Action Words

- jump
- run
- kick

The cheetah can ____________________ fast.

Watch the kangaroo ____________________.

The bear will ____________________ the ball.

NAME ____________________

Review

Pick the correct position word for each sentence.

Position Words	beside	on

The cat is ____________ the box.

The cat is ____________ the box.

Write two words that best describe your pet.

Describing Words	sad	happy	soft	hard

____________ ____________

Circle the correct order word.

first	next	I get dressed.
first	next	I wake up.

NAME ______________________

Lesson 10 Family Words

Trace and write each family word.

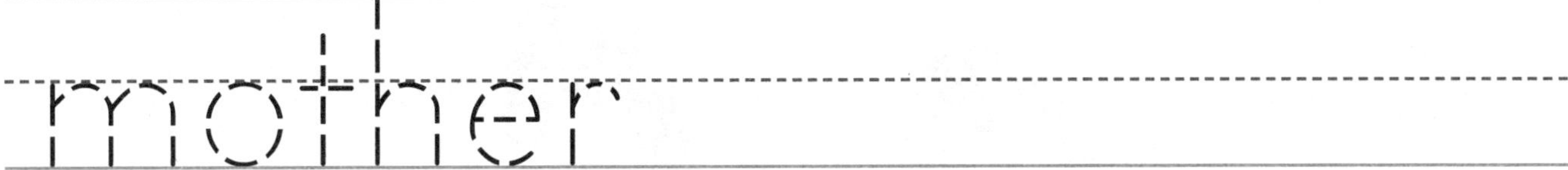

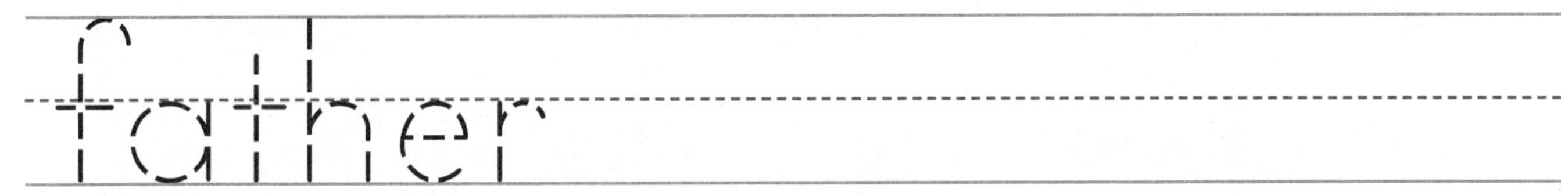

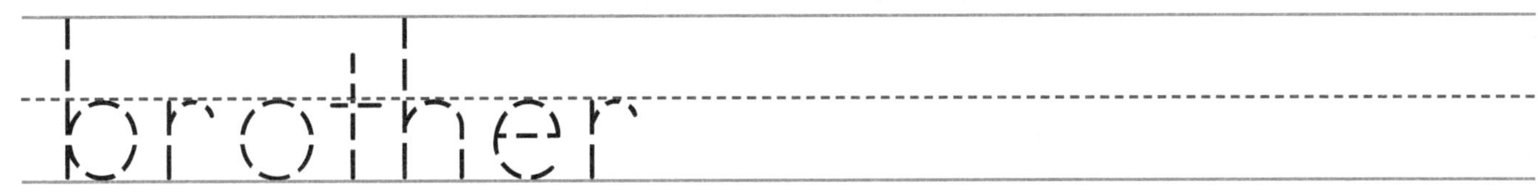

sister

Draw your family.

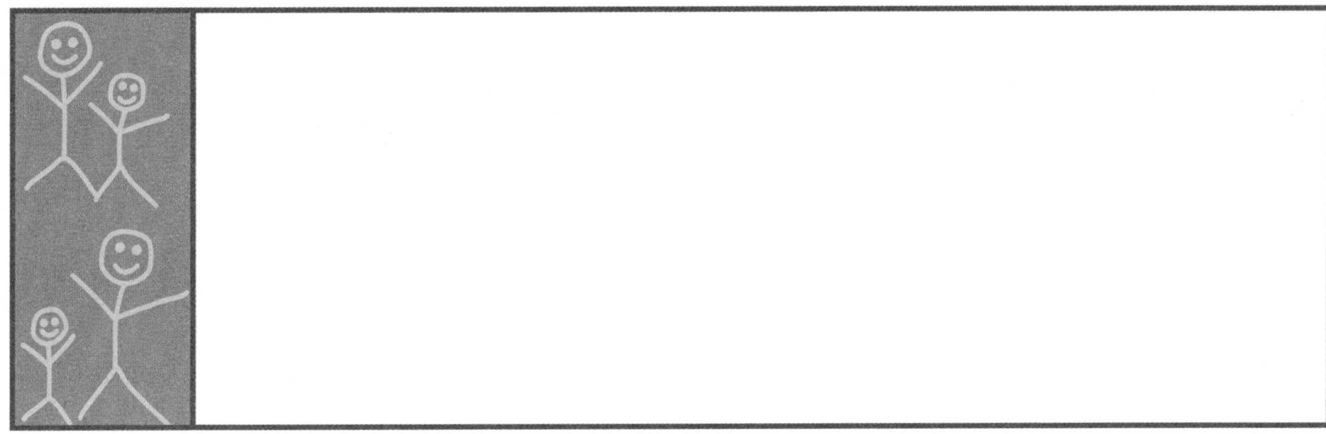

NAME ______________________

Lesson 10 Family Words

Look at the picture and write each family member correctly.

• The ______________________ is cooking.

• The ______________________ and

______________________ are playing a game.

• The ______________________ is pouring milk.

NAME ______________________

Lesson 11 Feeling Words

Trace and write each feeling word.

scared

sleepy

sad

NAME ____________________

Lesson 11 Feeling Words

Look at each picture. Write a word that tells how each person feels.

sad	sleepy	happy	scared

This girl is ____________________.

This boy looks ____________________.

This girl looks ____________________.

This boy is ____________________.

NAME ___________________________

Lesson 12 School Words

Trace and write each school word.

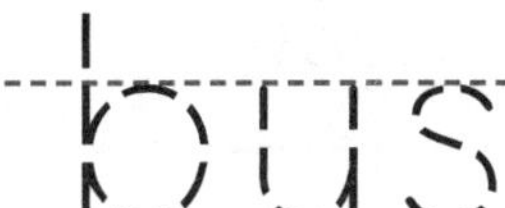

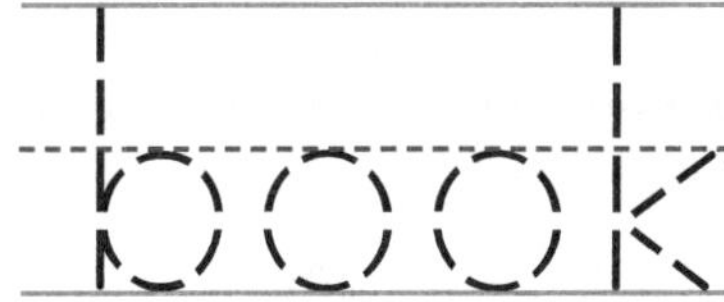

Write your teacher's name.

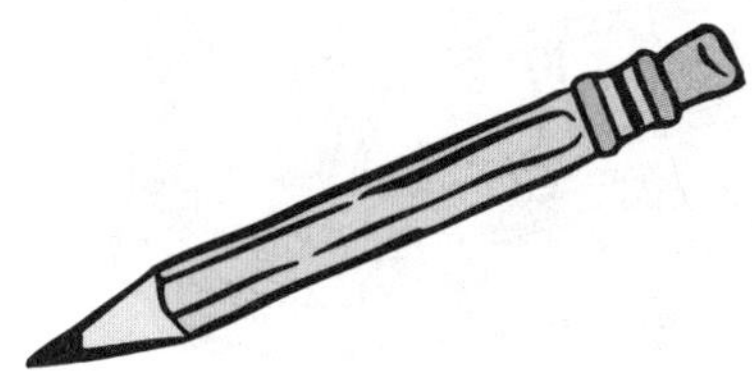

NAME ______________________

Lesson 12 School Words

Pick the correct word from the box. Write it on the line.

pencil	teacher	bus	book

NAME ______________________

Lesson 13 Animal Words

Trace and write each animal word.

cat

dog

horse

NAME ______________________

Lesson 13 Animal Words

Pick the correct word from the box. Write it on the line.

cat	dog	duck	horse

NAME ____________________

Review

Write the correct words under each heading.

mother	horse	sleepy	paper	book	cat	sad	sister

Family

____________________ ____________________

School

____________________ ____________________

Animal

____________________ ____________________

Feeling

____________________ ____________________

NAME ____________________

Review

Write the correct words beside each picture.

pencil	duck	brother	bus	dog	father	happy	scared

NAME ______________________________

Chapter 3 Post-Test

Draw an action. Name the action.

Draw and color a shape. Name the color and shape.

Draw an animal. Name the animal.

Draw a picture of you. Name your feeling.

Chapter 4

NAME ________________________________

Lesson 1 Sequencing

Label each story in order. Use the words **first**, **next**, and **last**.

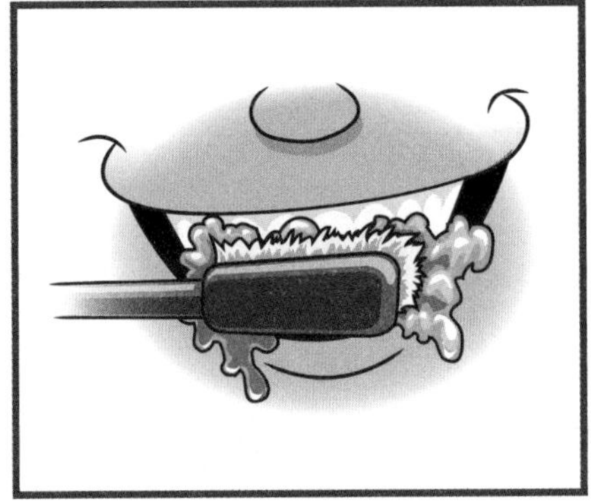

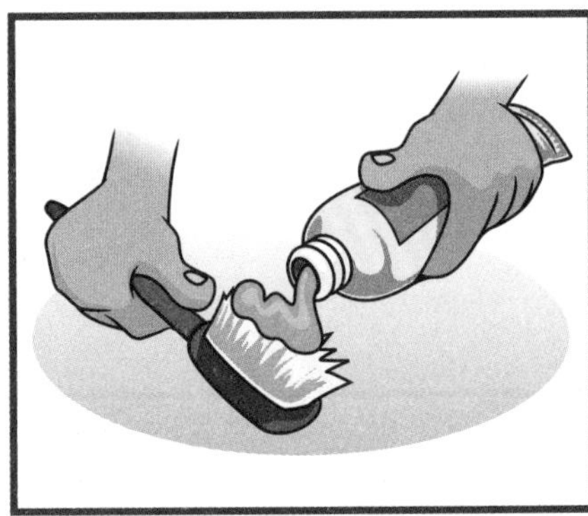

NAME ______________________

Lesson 2 Sequencing

Draw the missing picture to finish each story. Then, label the pictures in order using **first**, **next**, and **last**.

NAME ______________________

Lesson 3 Sequencing

Draw what might have happened after Kaeden saw the cake. Write **first** or **next** under each picture.

Draw what might have happened before Lauren dropped her ice cream. Write **first** or **next** under each picture.

NAME ______________________

Chapter 4 Post-Test

Draw pictures that tell about your day. Draw what you did **first, next,** and **last**. Write the order under each picture.

Chapter 5

NAME ______________________

Lesson 1 Story Starters

Read the beginning of each sentence. Then, finish each one.

I like school because ______________________

______________________ is my best friend because

NAME ______________________

Lesson 2 Story Starters

Read the beginning of each sentence. Then, finish each one.

If I had a pet dinosaur ______________________

I was sad when ______________________

NAME ______________________________

Chapter 5 Post-Test

Read the beginning of a story. Then, finish the story and draw a picture of it.

One day, my dog suddenly grew wings.

Chapter 6

NAME ____________________

Lesson 1 Letter Parts

A **friendly letter** has five parts. Trace each part of the following friendly letter.

NAME ______________________

Lesson 2 Friendly Letter

Fill in each missing part of the friendly letter.

____

____

Dear ______________________,

Did you have fun today? I did! It was

____

fun because ______________________

____

____

Love,

____

NAME ______________________________

Chapter 6 Post-Test

Draw a line to match each part of a friendly letter. Then, trace the name of each part.

June 1, 2015

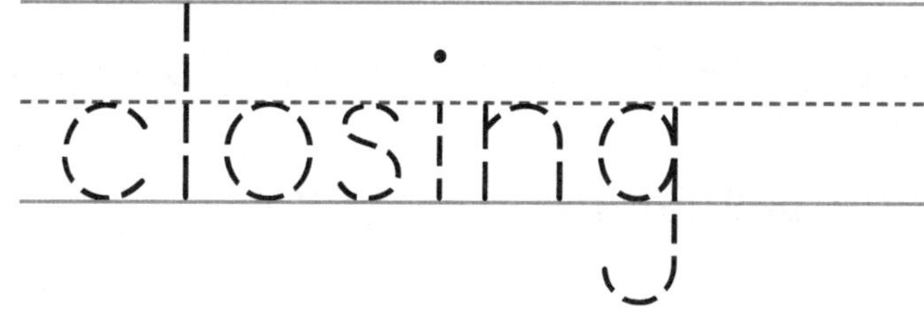

Dear Ava,

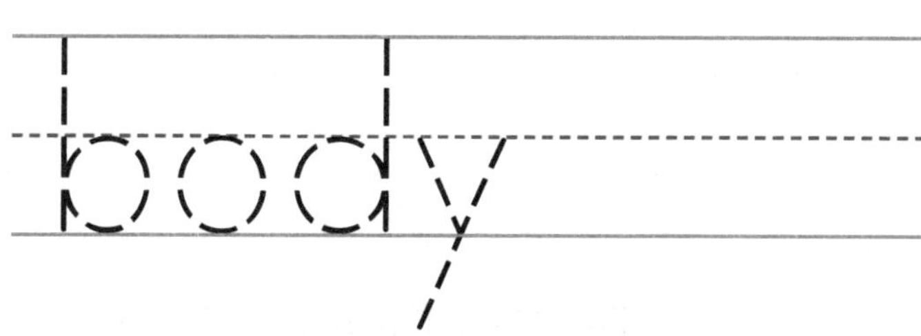

I was happy to see you last week.

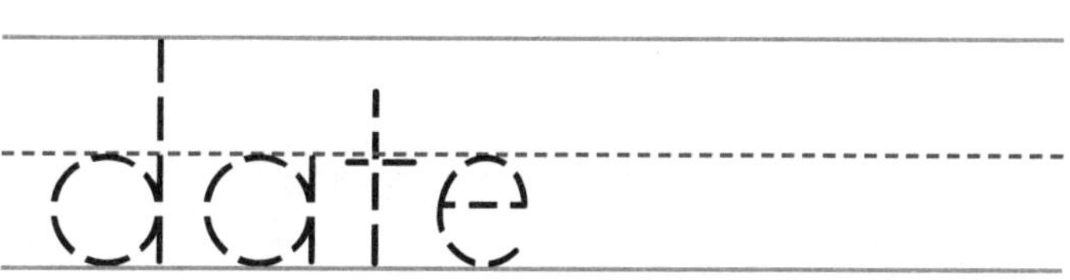

Your friend,

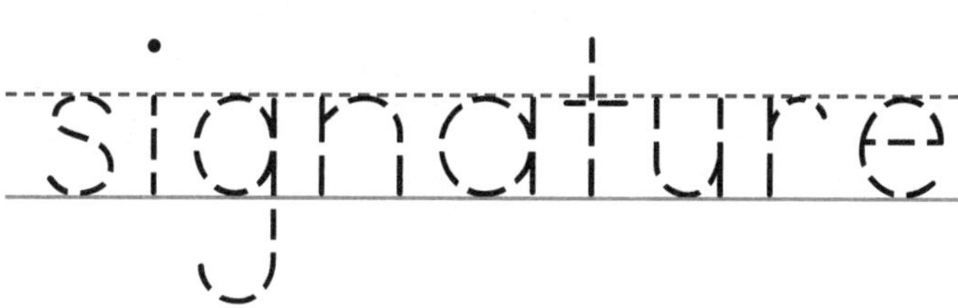

Cara

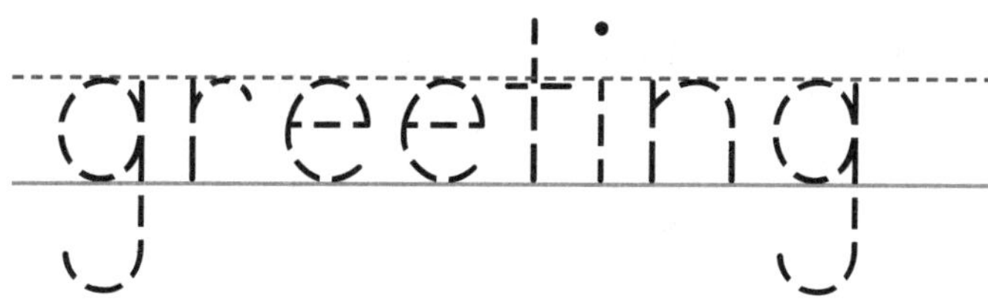

Chapter 7

NAME ______________________

Lesson 1 Telling Sentences

Sentences are made up of words that make sense when put together. Sentences that give us information begin with a capital letter and end with a period.

Copy each sentence. Begin each one with a capital letter and end each one with a period.

We went to the zoo.

We saw tigers and bears.

The train ride was fun.

The monkey was sleeping.

NAME ______________________

Lesson 2 Questions

A question is a sentence that asks a question and ends with a question mark.

Copy each sentence. Begin each one with a capital letter. End each one with a question mark.

Do you like to shop?

Where do you go?

What do you buy?

Do you have fun?

NAME ______________________

Chapter 7 Post-Test

All sentences begin with a capital letter and end with an end mark.

Write each sentence correctly.

1. Did you go.

2. I was on the bus

3. i did not see you.

4. were you hiding?

5. i will see you soon

NAME ____________________

Lesson 1 Word Web

The **main idea** of a story tells what the story is about. The **details** give more information about the main idea.

A **word web** will help the writer decide the main idea and details of a story.

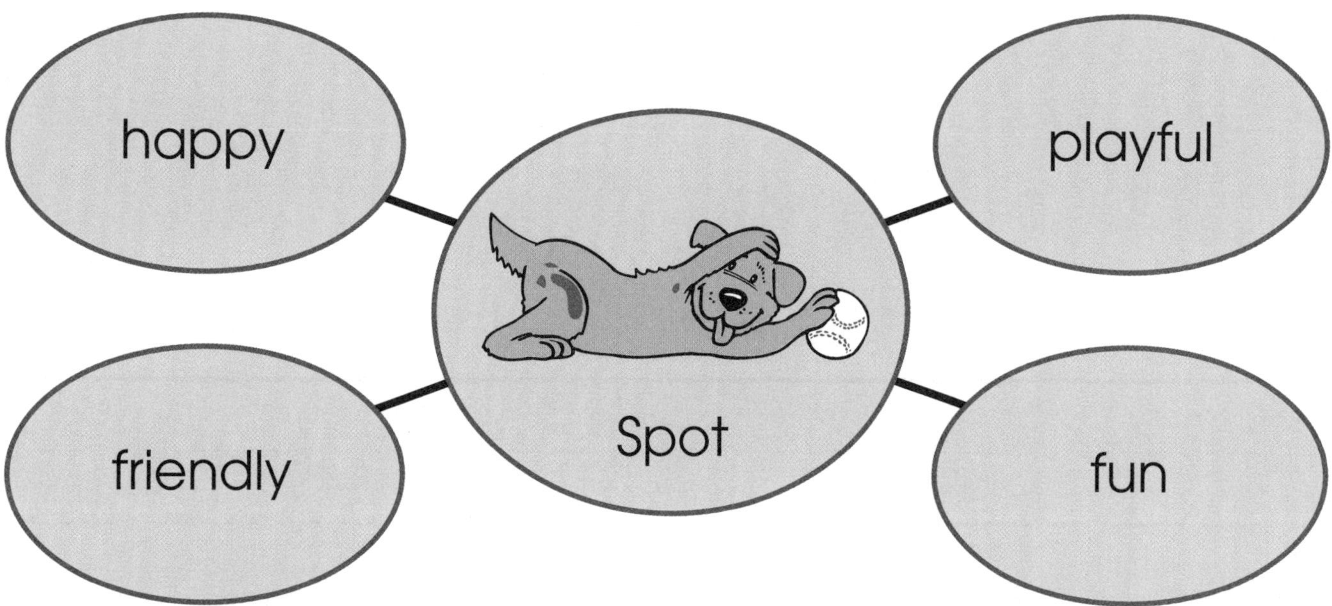

Now, make a word web about you.

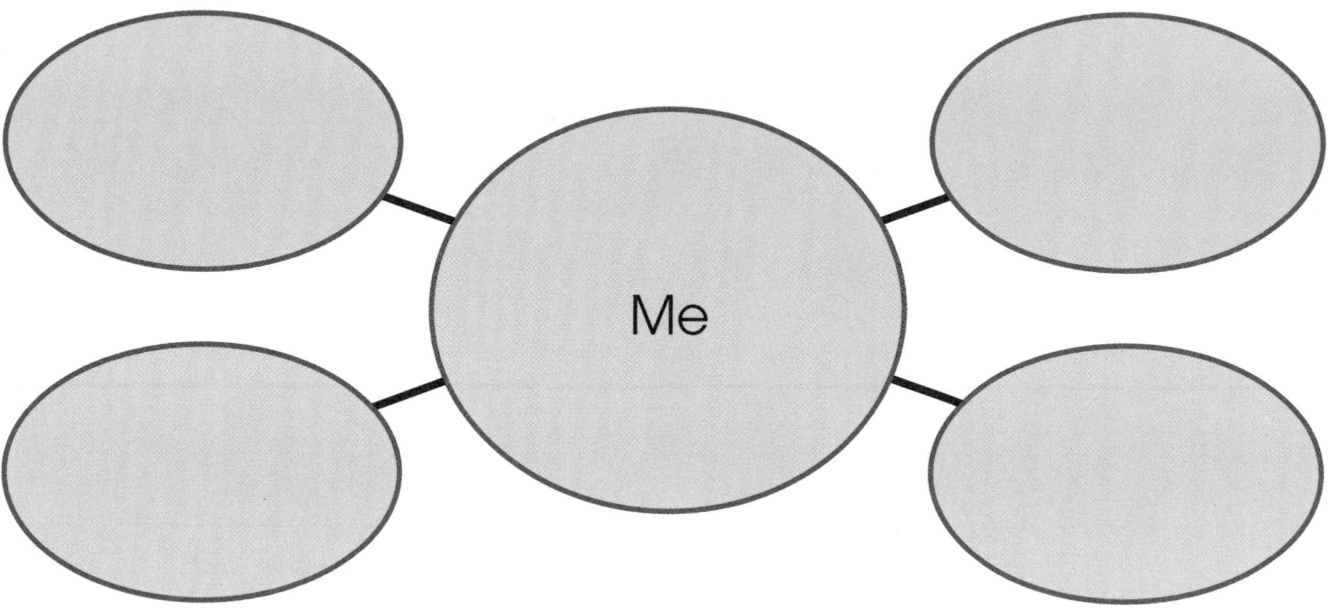

NAME ______________________

Lesson 2 Details

Choose a detail from the word web on page 91 labeled "Me" and write it under a box. Then, draw a picture of you that shows that detail. Choose another detail for the other box.

NAME ____________________

Lesson 2 Details

Choose the last two details about yourself. Write each one under a box. Then, draw a picture for each detail.

NAME ______________________________

Lesson 3 Main Idea and Details

Look back at pages 92 and 93. Write a complete sentence for each detail that tells about you.

Begin each sentence with a capital letter and end with an end mark.

NAME ___________________________

Lesson 4 Story

Write a story about yourself using some of your sentences from page 94. Then, write a title and draw a picture to go with your story.

Title

NAME ______________________________

Chapter 8 Post-Test

Make a word web. Write the name of an animal in the center of the web. Then, write one detail about the animal on each line.

NAME ______________________

Chapter 8 Post-Test

Use the details on your word web on page 96 to help you write a story about an animal. Then, write a title and draw a picture for your story.

Title

Chapter 9

NAME ______________________

Lesson 1 Rhyming Words

Rhyming words have the same ending sound. **Up** and **pup** are examples of words that rhyme. Many poems have words that rhyme.

Say the name of each picture on the left. Then, draw a line to the picture it rhymes with on the right.

tree

coat

frog

house

mouse

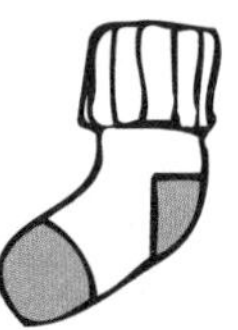

sock

goat

bee

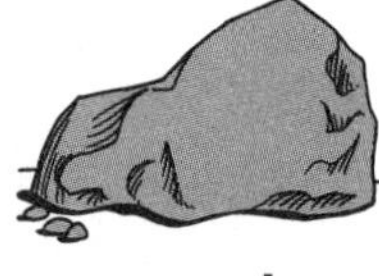

rock

dog

NAME ____________________

Lesson 2 Rhyming Words

Choose the correct rhyming words to complete the poem.

me	see	tree	flee	bee

A bird sat in a ____________________

to see what it could ____________________ .

Then, along came a ____________________

and the bird started to ____________________ .

It was all very surprising to ____________________ .

NAME ______________________

Chapter 9 Post-Test

Look at each picture. Then, complete each sentence using the rhyming words. Be sure to begin each sentence with a capital letter and end each one with a period.

goat	box	truck	fox	house	coat	duck	mouse

The fox sits on a box.

A ______________ has on a ______________.

The ______________ is on a ______________.

The ______________ is in a ______________.

NAME ______________________

Writer's Handbook Sentence Starters

Sentence starters help you begin a story.

If I found a cat, I would . . . . .

My birthday wish is . . . .

I wish I could go on a trip to . . . .

When I woke up today, I . . . .

I had a good time when . . . .

I was mad when . . . .

If I could fly . . . .

My favorite thing to do is . . . .

NAME ______________________

Writer's Handbook Sentences

Always begin each sentence with a capital letter and end each one with the correct end mark.

When writing a **telling sentence**, start with a capital letter and end with a period.

We rode the bus**.**

Spot likes to play**.**

Amy walked home**.**

When writing a **question**, begin with a capital letter and end with a question mark.

Did you ride the bus**?**

What does Spot like to play**?**

Did Amy walk home**?**

A sentence should always make sense. Complete sentences tell whom each sentence is about and what happened.

WHO?	**WHAT HAPPENED?**
The dog	barked.
My uncle	took me to the zoo.
Amy	went to school.

NAME ____________________

Writer's Handbook The Writing Process

Writers use five steps to write a story—prewrite, first draft, revise, proofread, publish.

Step 1: Prewrite

First, writers **prewrite**. They make a list of ideas they might like to write about. Then, they choose one idea from their list and put that idea in the center of a word web. This idea will be the **main idea** of their story. Next, writers add lines to their word web to write their story **details**.

For example, Ava wants to write about a trip to the park, so she made the following word web.

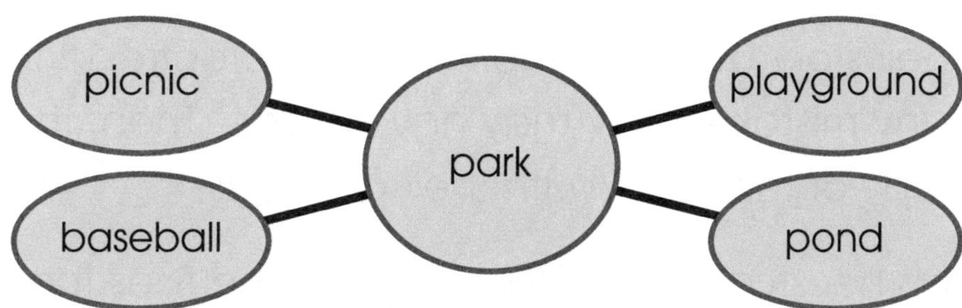

Step 2: First Draft

Then, writers write a **first draft** of their story using the information on their word web. They write a sentence for each detail.

Here is Ava's first draft.

I played on the slide. We threw the baseball. We watched ducks on the pond. We had a picnic.

NAME ___________________________

Writer's Handbook The Writing Process

Step 3: Revise

Next, writers read over their first draft to see if they can make it better.

Ava decides to make some changes, or **revise** her first draft. She wants to add more information to her details and a title.

Fun at the Park

First, Then, also
I played on the slide. We threw the baseball. We watched ducks
swim before leaving,
on the pond. We had a picnic.

Step 4: Proofread

Writers read their story over one more time, or proofread their story. They look for any mistakes they may have made. Then, they make a neat, clean copy of their story with their changes.

Ava proofreads her story to look for mistakes. She fixes the mistakes and writes a new copy. She makes sure her writing is neat.

Fun at the Park

First, I played on the slide. Then, we threw the baseball. We also watched ducks swim on the pond. Before leaving, we had a picnic.

Step 5: Publish

Finally, writers **publish** their stories. They can add pictures and make a book or poster to share with others. Ava made a book that she could read out loud.

Answer Key

Aa

Amy

acorn

Trace the letter **A**.

A A A A A A

Write the letter **A**.

A A A A A A

Trace the letter **a**.

a a a a a a

Write the letter **a**.

a a a a a a

Spectrum Writing
Grade K

Chapter 1 Lesson 1
Writing Words

5

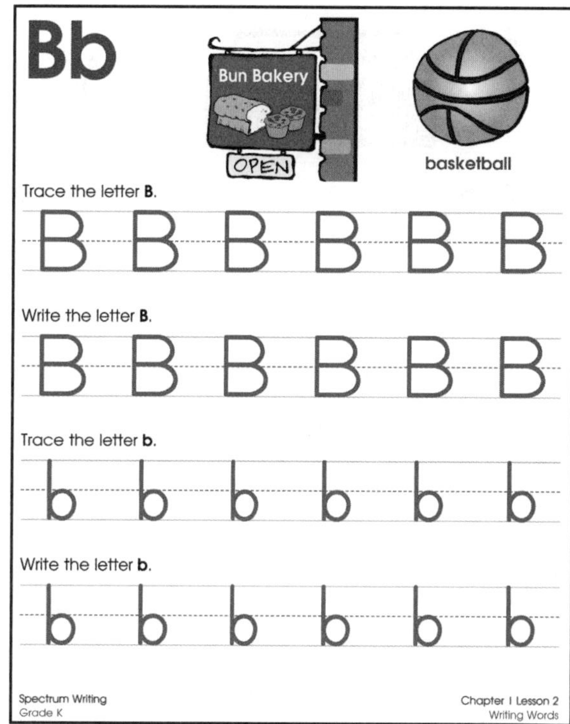
Bb

Bun Bakery

OPEN

basketball

Trace the letter **B**.

B B B B B B

Write the letter **B**.

B B B B B B

Trace the letter **b**.

b b b b b b

Write the letter **b**.

b b b b b b

Spectrum Writing
Grade K

Chapter 1 Lesson 2
Writing Words

6

Cc

Cory

cat

Trace the letter **C**.

C C C C C C

Write the letter **C**.

C C C C C C

Trace the letter **c**.

c c c c c c

Write the letter **c**.

c c c c c c

Spectrum Writing
Grade K

Chapter 1 Lesson 3
Writing Words

7

Dd

Dr. Davis

dog

Trace the letter **D**.

D D D D D D

Write the letter **D**.

D D D D D D

Trace the letter **d**.

d d d d d d

Write the letter **d**.

d d d d d d

Spectrum Writing
Grade K

Chapter 1 Lesson 4
Writing Words

8

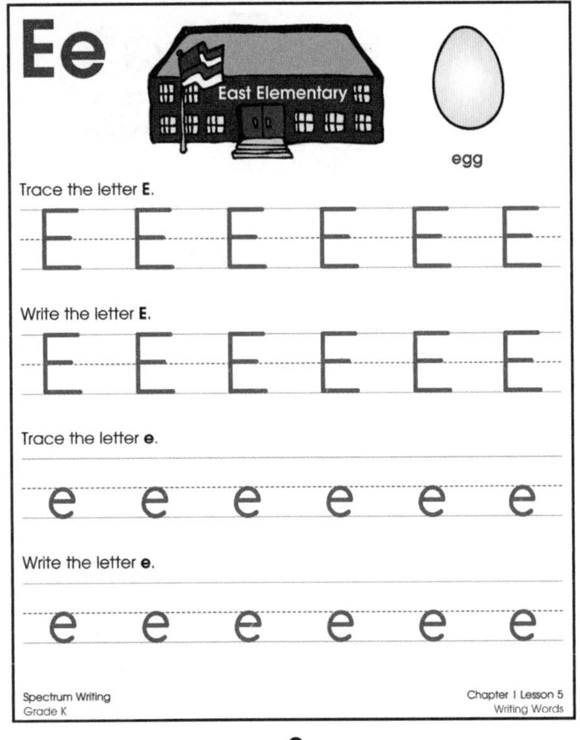
Ee
East Elementary
egg
Trace the letter E.
E E E E E E
Write the letter E.
E E E E E E
Trace the letter e.
e e e e e e
Write the letter e.
e e e e e e
Spectrum Writing
Grade K
Chapter 1 Lesson 5
Writing Words

9

Ff
Frank
fish
Trace the letter F.
F F F F F F
Write the letter F.
F F F F F F
Trace the letter f.
f f f f f f
Write the letter f.
f f f f f f
Spectrum Writing
Grade K
Chapter 1 Lesson 6
Writing Words

10

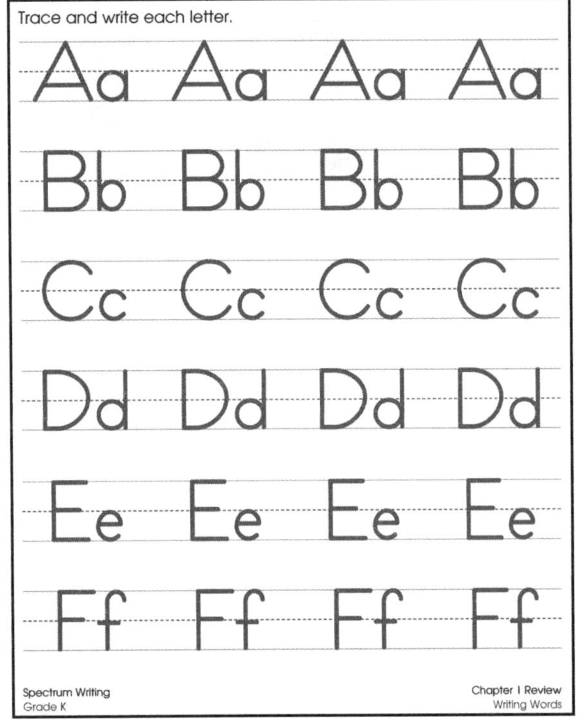
Trace and write each letter.
Aa Aa Aa Aa
Bb Bb Bb Bb
Cc Cc Cc Cc
Dd Dd Dd Dd
Ee Ee Ee Ee
Ff Ff Ff Ff
Spectrum Writing
Grade K
Chapter 1 Review
Writing Words

11

Gg
Gabe's Garden
goose
Trace the letter G.
G G G G G G
Write the letter G.
G G G G G G
Trace the letter g.
g g g g g g
Write the letter g.
g g g g g g
Spectrum Writing
Grade K
Chapter 1 Lesson 7
Writing Words

12

Answer Key

13

14

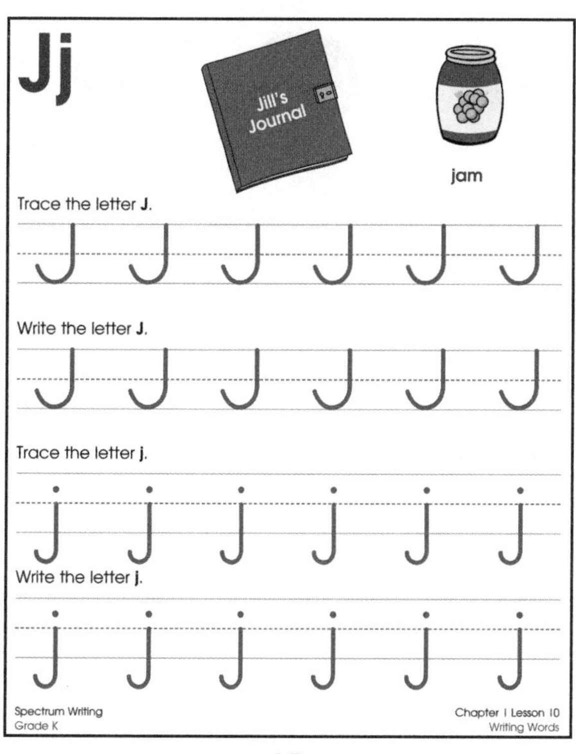

15

16

Answer Key

Ll

leaf

Trace the letter **L**.

L L L L L L

Write the letter **L**.

L L L L L L

Trace the letter **l**.

l l l l l l

Write the letter **l**.

l l l l l l

Spectrum Writing
Grade K

Chapter 1 Lesson 12
Writing Words

17

Trace and write each letter.

Gg Gg Gg Gg

Hh Hh Hh Hh

Ii Ii Ii Ii

Jj Jj Jj Jj

Kk Kk Kk Kk

Ll Ll Ll Ll

Spectrum Writing
Grade K

Chapter 1 Review
Writing Words

18

Mm

Mr. Mack

mouse

Trace the letter **M**.

M M M M M M

Write the letter **M**.

M M M M M M

Trace the letter **m**.

m m m m m m

Write the letter **m**.

m m m m m m

Spectrum Writing
Grade K

Chapter 1 Lesson 13
Writing Words

19

Nn

nut

Trace the letter **N**.

N N N N N N

Write the letter **N**.

N N N N N N

Trace the letter **n**.

n n n n n n

Write the letter **n**.

n n n n n n

Spectrum Writing
Grade K

Chapter 1 Lesson 14
Writing Words

20

Oo

Omeka's Olives

octopus

Trace the letter **O**.

O O O O O O

Write the letter **O**.

O O O O O O

Trace the letter **o**.

o o o o o o

Write the letter **o**.

o o o o o o

Spectrum Writing
Grade K

Chapter 1 Lesson 15
Writing Words

21

Pp

Pablo for President

Pig

Trace the letter **P**.

P P P P P P

Write the letter **P**.

P P P P P P

Trace the letter **p**.

p p p p p p

Write the letter **p**.

p p p p p p

Spectrum Writing
Grade K

Chapter 1 Lesson 16
Writing Words

22

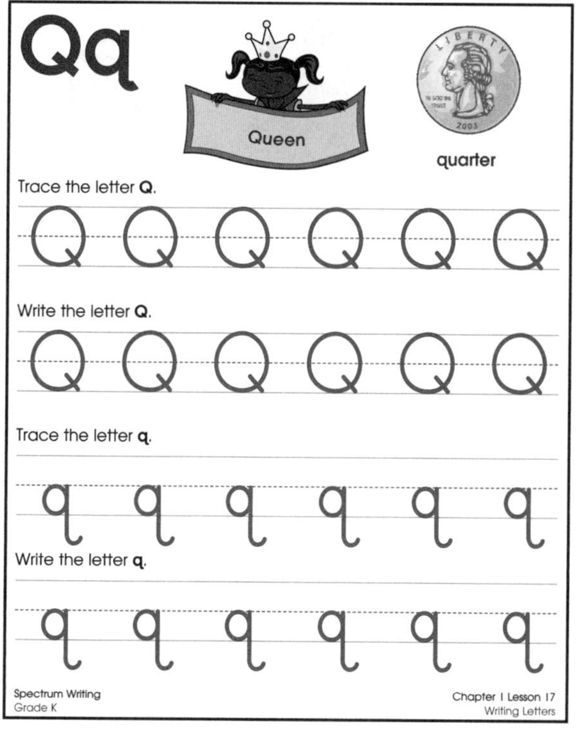
Qq

Queen

quarter

Trace the letter **Q**.

Q Q Q Q Q Q

Write the letter **Q**.

Q Q Q Q Q Q

Trace the letter **q**.

q q q q q q

Write the letter **q**.

q q q q q q

Spectrum Writing
Grade K

Chapter 1 Lesson 17
Writing Letters

23

Rr

Rabbit Road

ring

Trace the letter **R**.

R R R R R R

Write the letter **R**.

R R R R R R

Trace the letter **r**.

r r r r r r

Write the letter **r**.

r r r r r r

Spectrum Writing
Grade K

Chapter 1 Lesson 18
Writing Words

24

Ss

Sam's Sunflower Seeds

sun

Trace the letter **S**.

S S S S S S

Write the letter **S**.

S S S S S S

Trace the letter **s**.

s s s s s s

Write the letter **s**.

s s s s s s

Spectrum Writing
Grade K

Chapter 1 Lesson 19
Writing Words

25

Trace and write each letter.

Mm Mm Mm Mm

Nn Nn Nn Nn

Oo Oo Oo Oo

Pp Pp Pp Pp

Qq Qq Qq Qq

Rr Rr Rr Rr

Ss Ss Ss Ss

Spectrum Writing
Grade K

Chapter 1 Review
Writing Words

26

Tt

Tyrone

turtle

Trace the letter **T**.

T T T T T T

Write the letter **T**.

T T T T T T

Trace the letter **t**.

t t t t t t

Write the letter **t**.

t t t t t t

Spectrum Writing
Grade K

Chapter 1 Lesson 20
Writing Words

27

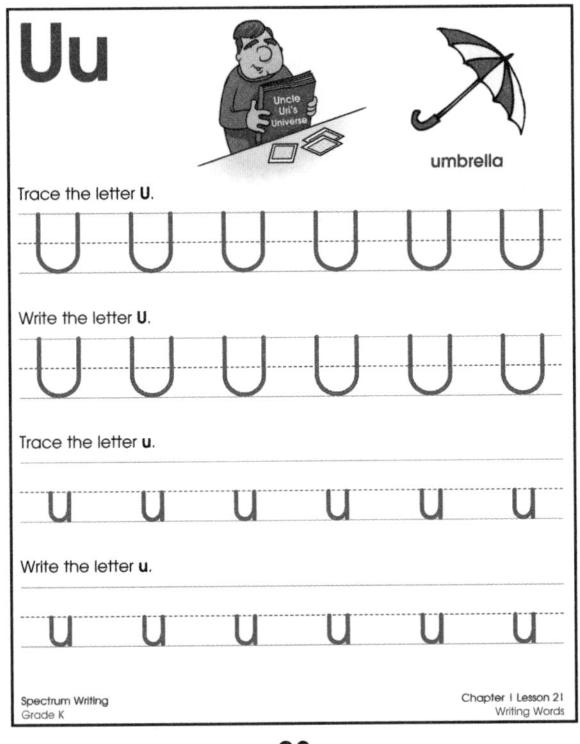

Uu

Uncle Uri's Universe

umbrella

Trace the letter **U**.

U U U U U U

Write the letter **U**.

U U U U U U

Trace the letter **u**.

u u u u u u

Write the letter **u**.

u u u u u u

Spectrum Writing
Grade K

Chapter 1 Lesson 21
Writing Words

28

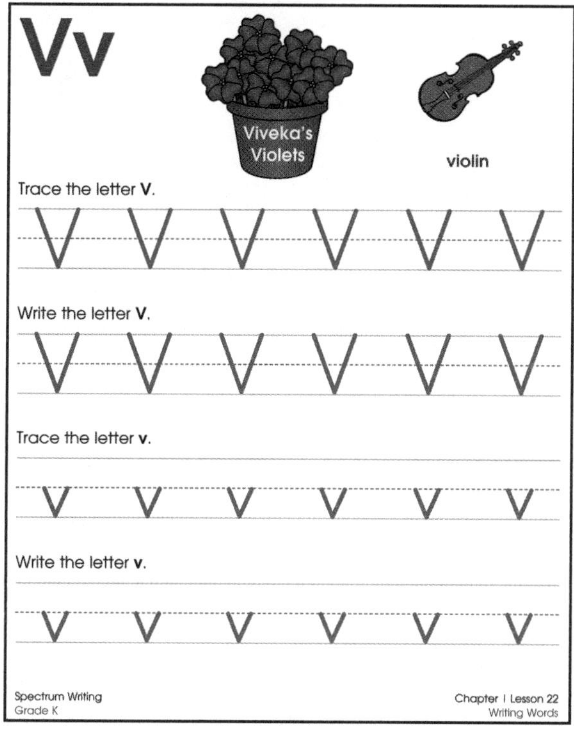
Vv
Viveka's
Violets
violin
Trace the letter V.
V V V V V V
Write the letter V.
V V V V V V
Trace the letter v.
v v v v v v
Write the letter v.
v v v v v v
Spectrum Writing
Grade K
Chapter 1 Lesson 22
Writing Words

29

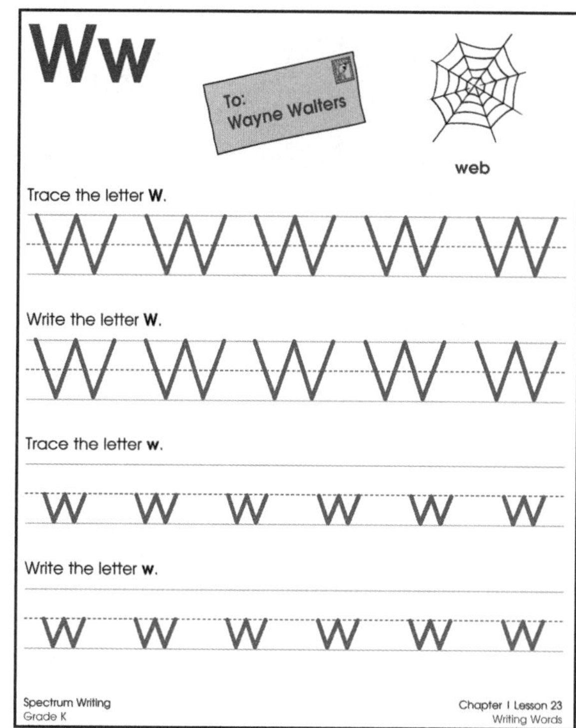
Ww
To:
Wayne Walters
web
Trace the letter W.
W W W W W
Write the letter W.
W W W W W
Trace the letter w.
w w w w w w
Write the letter w.
w w w w w w
Spectrum Writing
Grade K
Chapter 1 Lesson 23
Writing Words

30

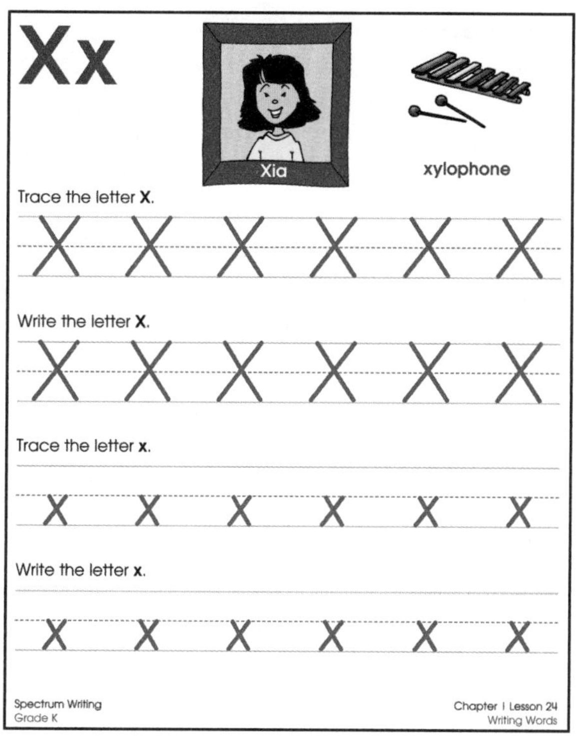
Xx
Xia
xylophone
Trace the letter X.
X X X X X X
Write the letter X.
X X X X X X
Trace the letter x.
x x x x x x
Write the letter x.
x x x x x x
Spectrum Writing
Grade K
Chapter 1 Lesson 24
Writing Words

31

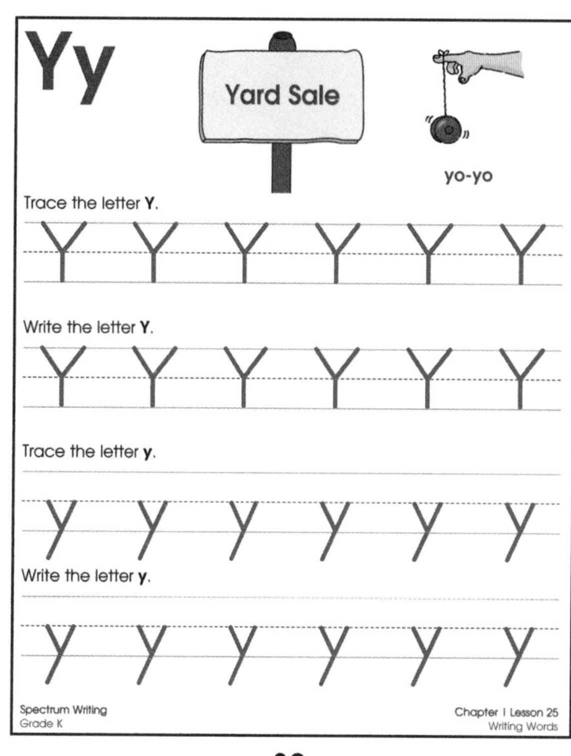
Yy
Yard Sale
yo-yo
Trace the letter Y.
Y Y Y Y Y Y
Write the letter Y.
Y Y Y Y Y Y
Trace the letter y.
y y y y y y
Write the letter y.
y y y y y y
Spectrum Writing
Grade K
Chapter 1 Lesson 25
Writing Words

32

Answer Key

33

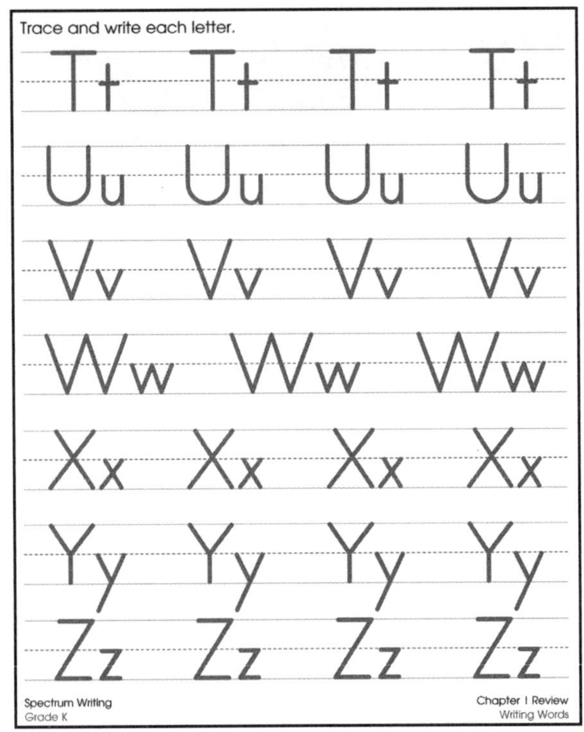

34

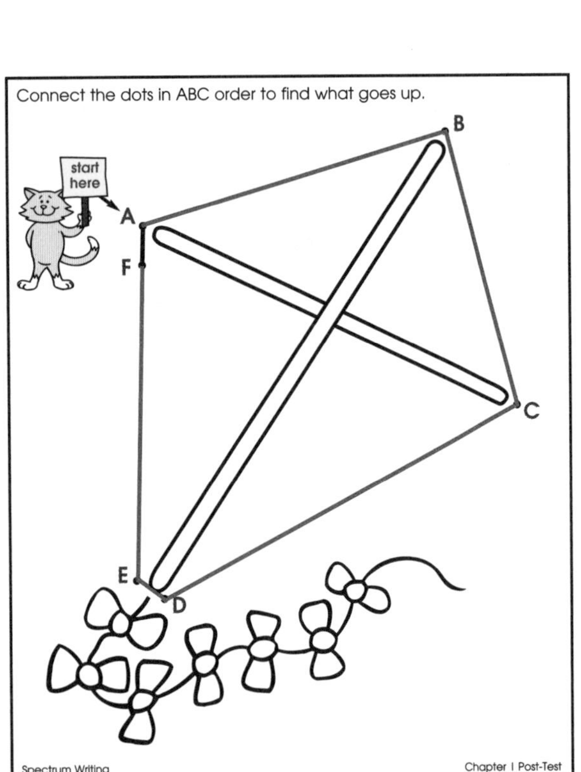

35

36

Answer Key

Write the name of your pet. Then, draw a picture of it.

My pet's name is

Answers will vary.

Drawings will vary.

Spectrum Writing
Grade K

Chapter 2 Lesson 2
All About Me

37

Write the name of your favorite food. Then, draw it in the box.

My favorite food is

Answers will vary.

Drawings will vary.

Spectrum Writing
Grade K

Chapter 2 Lesson 3
All About Me

38

Write it the name of your favorite toy. Then, draw it in the box.

My favorite toy is

Answers will vary.

Drawings will vary.

Spectrum Writing
Grade K

Chapter 2 Lesson 4
All About Me

39

Write the name of your teacher. Then, draw a picture of your teacher.

My teacher's name is

Answers will vary.

Drawings will vary.

Spectrum Writing
Grade K

Chapter 2 Lesson 5
All About Me

40

Answer Key

Write your friend's name. Then, draw a picture of your friend.

My friend's name is

Answers will vary.

Drawings will vary.

Spectrum Writing
Grade K

Chapter 2 Lesson 6
All About Me

41

Write the names of the people in your family. Then, draw your family.

The names of the people in my family are

Answers will vary.

Drawings will vary.

Spectrum Writing
Grade K

Chapter 2 Lesson 7
All About Me

42

Write your address. Then, draw your home.

My address is

Answers will vary.

Drawings will vary.

Spectrum Writing
Grade K

Chapter 2 Lesson 8
All About Me

43

Write about something you like to do. Then, draw yourself doing it.

I like to

Answers will vary.

Drawings will vary.

Spectrum Writing
Grade K

Chapter 2 Post-Test
All About Me

44

Answer Key

Trace and write each color word.

blue blue

yellow yellow

green green

red red

orange orange

purple purple

Spectrum Writing
Grade K

Chapter 3 Lesson 1
Story Words

45

Write the word from the box that names the color of each picture.

red green blue yellow purple orange

green | red

yellow | blue

orange | purple

Spectrum Writing
Grade K

Chapter 3 Lesson 1
Story Words

46

Trace and write each shape word.

circle circle

triangle triangle

rectanglerectangle

square square

oval oval

heart heart

Spectrum Writing
Grade K

Chapter 3 Lesson 2
Story Words

47

Write the word that names each shape.

circle oval square rectangle triangle heart

rectangle | heart

square | triangle

circle | oval

Spectrum Writing
Grade K

Chapter 3 Lesson 2
Story Words

48

Answer Key

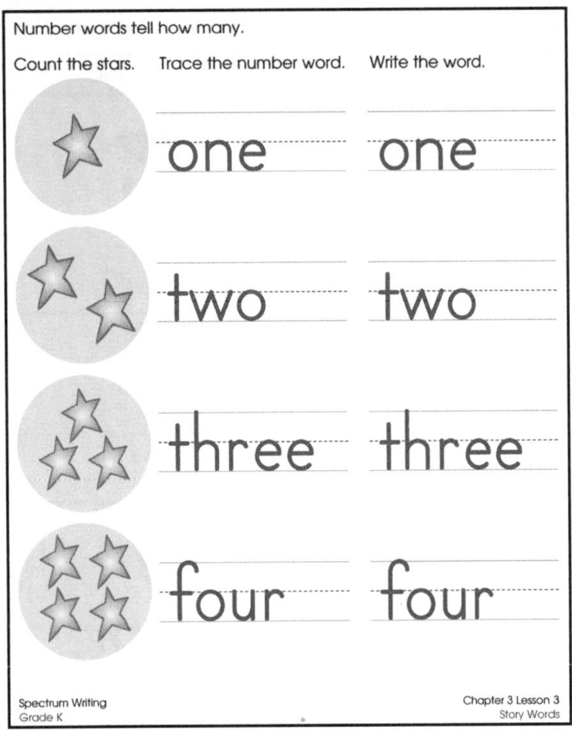

Number words tell how many.

Count the stars. Trace the number word. Write the word.

one one

two two

three three

four four

Spectrum Writing
Grade K

Chapter 3 Lesson 3
Story Words

49

Number words tell how many.

Count the stars. Trace the number word. Write the word.

five five

six six

seven seven

eight eight

Spectrum Writing
Grade K

Chapter 3 Lesson 3
Story Words

50

Trace and write each size word.

The dinosaur is big. big

The mouse is small. small

The tree is tall. tall

The bush is short. short

Spectrum Writing
Grade K

Chapter 3 Lesson 4
Story Words

51

Write the correct size word on each line.

tall short

short tall tall

big small

small big small

Draw something tall. Draw something small.

Drawings will vary.

Spectrum Writing
Grade K

Chapter 3 Lesson 4
Story Words

52

Answer Key

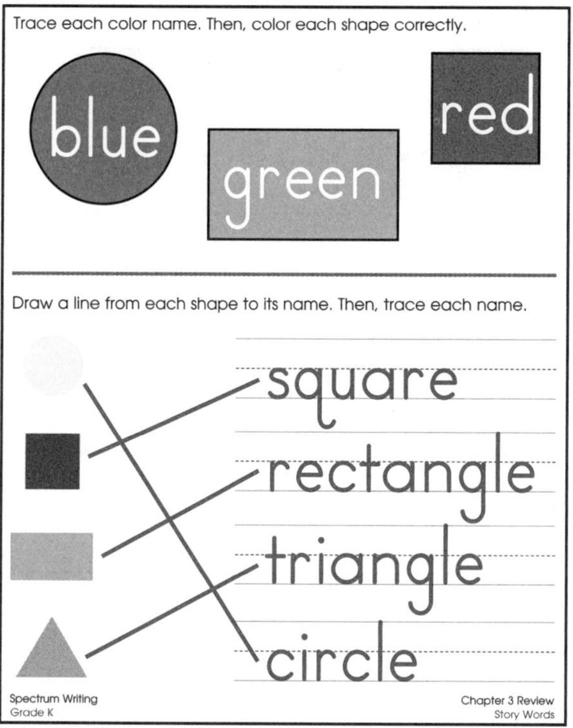

Trace each color name. Then, color each shape correctly.

blue green red

Draw a line from each shape to its name. Then, trace each name.

square
rectangle
triangle
circle

Spectrum Writing
Grade K

Chapter 3 Review
Story Words

53

Count the balloons. Then, write the number on the line.

five two seven

Circle the **big** tiger. Then, write **big**.

big

Circle the **short** tree. Then, write **short**.

short

Circle the **tall** man. Then, write **tall**.

tall

Circle the **small** sandwich. Then, write **small**.

small

Spectrum Writing
Grade K

Chapter 3 Review
Story Words

54

A naming word names a person, place, or thing.

Trace and write each naming word.

person person
place place
thing thing

Person? Place? Thing? Write the correct answer.

thing person place

Spectrum Writing
Grade K

Chapter 3 Lesson 5
Naming Words

55

Write the correct naming word under each picture.

person	place	thing

place thing
person thing
place person

Spectrum Writing
Grade K

Chapter 3 Lesson 5
Story Words

56

Answer Key

57

Write the action word that goes with each picture.

run	throw	kick	jump

run

jump

kick

throw

Answers will vary.

Which action do you like to do?

Spectrum Writing
Grade K

Chapter 3 Lesson 6
Story Words

58

Position words tell where things are located.

Trace and then write each position word.

The boy is in the bed. is

Fluffy is jumping over the mouse. over

The mouse is on the drum. on

The calf is beside the cow. beside

Spot is under the table. under

Spectrum Writing
Grade K

Chapter 3 Lesson 7
Story Words

59

Write the correct position word to show where the mouse is.

under	over	in	beside	on

in

on

under

beside

over

Draw a worm in an apple.

Drawings will vary.

Spectrum Writing
Grade K

Chapter 3 Lesson 7
Story Words

60

Answer Key

Describing words tell how things look or feel.

Trace and write each describing word.

The movie made Lauren sad. sad

Jose is a happy boy. happy

The rabbit is very soft. soft

My bat is hard. hard

Spectrum Writing
Grade K

Chapter 3 Lesson 8
Story Words

61

Write the describing word that tells about each picture.

happy	hard	sad	soft

The pillow is soft.

This is a happy face.

My desk is hard.

The story made me sad.

Spectrum Writing
Grade K

Chapter 3 Lesson 8
Story Words

62

Order words tell the order in which things happen.

Trace and write each order word.

First, get your paper and crayons. First

Next, draw your picture. Next

Last, hang up your picture. Last

Spectrum Writing
Grade K

Chapter 3 Lesson 9
Story Words

63

Write the describing word that goes with each picture.

first	next	last

first Lauren gets a hammer, nails, and wood.

last Lauren hangs the birdhouse in a tree.

next Lauren makes a birdhouse.

Spectrum Writing
Grade K

Chapter 3 Lesson 9
Story Words

64

Answer Key

Write the correct naming word to complete each sentence.

Naming Words
person
place
thing

The diving board is a thing.

The girl is a person.

The pool is a place.

Write the correct action word to complete each sentence.

Action Words
jump
run
kick

The cheetah can run fast.

Watch the kangaroo jump.

The bear will kick the ball.

Spectrum Writing
Grade K

Chapter 3 Review
Story Words

65

Pick the correct position word for each sentence.

Position Words	beside	on

The cat is on the box.

The cat is beside the box.

Write two words that best describe your pet.

Describing Words	sad	happy	soft	hard

Answers will vary.

Circle the correct order word.

first (next) — I get dressed.

(first) next — I wake up.

Spectrum Writing
Grade K

Chapter 3 Review
Story Words

66

Trace and write each family word.

mother mother

father father

brother brother

sister sister

Draw your family.

Drawings will vary.

Spectrum Writing
Grade K

Chapter 3 Lesson 10
Story Words

67

Look at the picture and write each family member correctly.

- The mother is cooking.
- The brother and sister are playing a game.
- The father is pouring milk.

Spectrum Writing
Grade K

Chapter 3 Lesson 10
Story Words

68

Answer Key

Trace and write each feeling word.

happy happy

scared scared

sleepy sleepy

sad sad

Spectrum Writing
Grade K

Chapter 3 Lesson 11
Story Words

69

Look at each picture. Write a word that tells how each person feels.

sad	sleepy	happy	scared

This girl is happy.

This boy looks sleepy.

This girl looks sad.

This boy is scared.

Spectrum Writing
Grade K

Chapter 3 Lesson 11
Story Words

70

Trace and write each school word.

bus bus

teacher teacher

pencil pencil

book book

Write your teacher's name.

Answers will vary.

Spectrum Writing
Grade K

Chapter 3 Lesson 12
Story Words

71

Pick the correct word from the box. Write it on the line.

pencil	teacher	bus	book

teacher

book

bus

pencil

Spectrum Writing
Grade K

Chapter 3 Lesson 12
Story Words

72

Answer Key

Trace and write each animal word.

duck duck

cat cat

dog dog

horse horse

Spectrum Writing
Grade K

Chapter 3 Lesson 13
Story Words

73

Spectrum Writing
Grade K

Chapter 3 Lesson 13
Story Words

74

Write the correct words under each heading.

mother horse sleepy paper book cat sad sister

Family

mother sister

School

paper book

Animal

horse cat

Feeling

sleepy sad

Spectrum Writing
Grade K

Chapter 3 Review
Story Words

75

Write the correct words beside each picture.

pencil duck brother bus dog father happy scared

happy brother

scared dog

man pencil

duck bus

Spectrum Writing
Grade K

Chapter 3 Review
Story Words

76

Answer Key

Draw an action. Name the action.

Drawings will vary. Answers will vary.

Draw and color a shape. Name the color and shape.

Drawings will vary. Answers will vary.

Draw an animal. Name the animal.

Drawings will vary. Answers will vary.

Draw a picture of you. Name your feeling.

Drawings will vary. Answers will vary.

Spectrum Writing
Grade K

Chapter 3 Post-Test
Story Words

77

Label each story in order. Use the words **first**, **next**, and **last**.

next first last

last next first

Spectrum Writing
Grade K

Chapter 4 Lesson 1
Sequencing

78

Draw the missing picture to finish each story. Then, label the pictures in order using **first**, **next**, and **last**.

boy reading book

first next last

girl making sandwich

first next last

Spectrum Writing
Grade K

Chapter 4 Lesson 2
Sequencing

79

Draw what might have happened after Kaeden saw the cake. Write **first** or **next** under each picture.

Possible picture: boy blowing out candles

first next

Draw what might have happened before Lauren dropped her ice cream. Write **first** or **next** under each picture.

Possible picture: girl eating ice cream cone

first next

Spectrum Writing
Grade K

Chapter 4 Lesson 3
Sequencing

80

Answer Key

Draw a story that tells about your day. Draw what you did **first**, **next**, and **last**. Write the order under each picture.

Drawings will vary.

first next last

Spectrum Writing
Grade K

Chapter 4 Post-Test
Sequencing

81

Read the beginning of each sentence. Then, finish each one.

I like school because

Sentence will vary.

is my best friend because

Sentence will vary.

Spectrum Writing
Grade K

Chapter 5 Lesson 1
Story Starters

82

Read the beginning of each sentence. Then, finish each one.

If I had a pet dinosaur

Sentence will vary.

I was sad when

Sentence will vary.

Spectrum Writing
Grade K

Chapter 5 Lesson 2
Story Starters

83

Read the beginning of a story. Then, finish the story and draw a picture of it.

One day my dog suddenly grew wings.

Stories will vary.

Drawings will vary.

Spectrum Writing
Grade K

Chapter 5 Post-Test
Story Starters

84

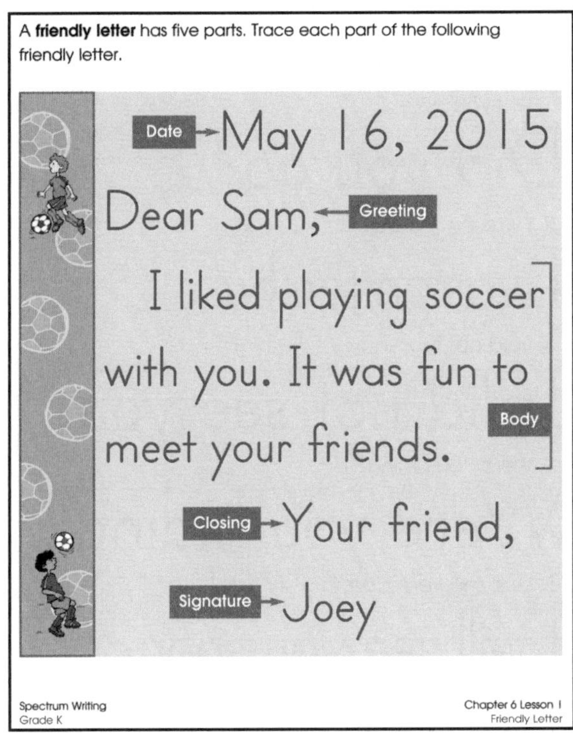

A **friendly letter** has five parts. Trace each part of the following friendly letter.

Date → May 16, 2015

Dear Sam, ← Greeting

I liked playing soccer with you. It was fun to meet your friends. — Body

Closing → Your friend,

Signature → Joey

Spectrum Writing
Grade K

Chapter 6 Lesson 1
Friendly Letter

85

Fill in each missing part of the friendly letter.

Letters will vary.

Dear ______,

Did you have fun today? I did! It was ______

fun because ______

Love,

Spectrum Writing
Grade K

Chapter 6 Lesson 2
Friendly Letter

86

Draw a line to match each part of a friendly letter. Then, trace the name of each part.

June 1, 2015	closing
Dear Ava,	body
I was happy to see you last week.	date
Your friend,	signature
Cara	greeting

Spectrum Writing
Grade K

Chapter 6 Post-Test
Friendly Letter

87

Sentences are made up of words that make sense when put together. Sentences that give us information begin with a capital letter and end with a period.

Copy each sentence. Begin each one with a capital letter and end each one with a period.

We went to the zoo.

We went to the zoo.

We saw tigers and bears.

We saw tigers and bears.

The train ride was fun.

The train ride was fun.

The monkey was sleeping.

The monkey was sleeping.

Spectrum Writing
Grade K

Chapter 7 Lesson 1
Sentences

88

A question is a sentence that asks a question and ends with a question mark.

Copy each sentence. Begin each one with a capital letter. End each one with a question mark.

Do you like to shop?

Do you like to shop?

Where do you like to go?

Where do you like to go?

What do you buy?

What do you buy?

Do you have fun?

Do you have fun?

Spectrum Writing
Grade K

Chapter 7 Lesson 2
Sentences

89

All sentences begin with a capital letter and end with an end mark.

Write each sentence correctly.

1. Did you go.

Did you go?

2. I was on the bus

I was on the bus.

3. i did not see you.

I did not see you.

4. were you hiding?

Were you hiding?

5. i will see you soon

I will see you soon.

Spectrum Writing
Grade K

Chapter 7 Post-Test
Sentences

90

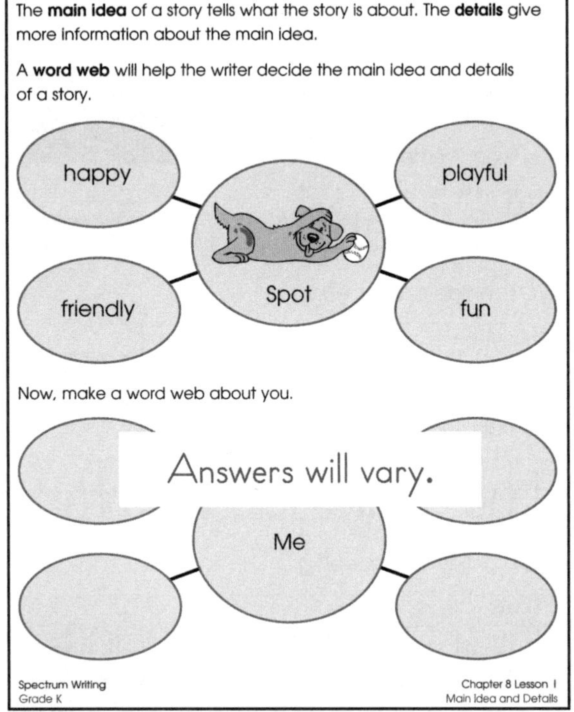

91

92

Answer Key

Choose the last two details about yourself. Write each one under a box. Then, draw a picture for each detail.

Drawings will vary.

Answers will vary.

Drawings will vary.

Answers will vary.

Spectrum Writing
Grade K

Chapter 8 Lesson 2
Main Idea and Details

93

Look back at pages 92 and 93. Write a complete sentence for each detail that tells about you.

Begin each sentence with a capital letter and end with an end mark.

Answers will vary.

Spectrum Writing
Grade K

Chapter 8 Lesson 3
Main Idea and Details

94

Write a story about yourself using some of your sentences from page 94. Then, write a title and draw a picture to go with your story.

Answers will vary.

Title

Drawings will vary.

Spectrum Writing
Grade K

Chapter 8 Lesson 4
Main Idea and Details

95

Make a word web. Write the name of an animal in the center of the web. Then, write one detail about the animal on each line.

Spectrum Writing
Grade K

Chapter 8 Post-Test
Main Idea and Details

96

Answer Key

Use the details on your word web on page 96 to help you write a story about an animal. Then, write a title and draw a picture for your story.

Answers will vary.

Title

Drawings will vary.

Spectrum Writing
Grade K

Chapter 8 Post-Test
Main Idea and Details

97

Rhyming words have the same ending sound. "Up" and "pup" are examples of words that rhyme. Many poems have words that rhyme.

Say the name of each picture on the left. Then, draw a line to the picture it rhymes with on the right.

- tree — bee
- frog — dog
- mouse — house
- goat — coat
- rock — sock

Spectrum Writing
Grade K

Chapter 9 Lesson 1
Poetry

98

Choose the correct rhyming words to complete the poem.

me see tree flee bee

A bird sat in a tree.

to see what it could see.

Then, along came a bee

and the bird started to flee.

It was all very surprising to me.

Spectrum Writing
Grade K

Chapter 9 Lesson 2
Poetry

99

Look at each picture. Then, complete each sentence using the rhyming words. Be sure to begin each sentence with a capital letter and end each one with a period.

goat box truck fox house coat duck mouse

The fox sits on a box.

A goat has on a coat.

The duck is on a truck.

The mouse is in a house.

Spectrum Writing
Grade K

Chapter 9 Post-Test
Poetry

100